THE PATH
OF THE
MEDICINE WHEEL

Kathy L. Callahan, Ph.D.

Affirmations By

Deirdre L. Aragon

Order this book online at www.trafford.com
or email orders@trafford.com

Most Trafford titles are also available at major online book retailers.

Published in conjunction with Spirit Song Publications

Printed in Victoria, BC, Canada.

ISBN: 978-1-4269-1628-1

*Our mission is to efficiently provide the world's finest, most comprehensive book publishing
service, enabling every author to experience success. To find out how to publish your book, your
way, and have it available worldwide, visit us online at www.trafford.com*

Trafford rev. 1/19/10

www.trafford.com

North America & international
toll-free: 1 888 232 4444 (USA & Canada)
phone: 250 383 6864 ♦ fax: 812 355 4082

Books by the Author

MultiSensory Human: The Evolution of the Soul, A.R.E. Press, 2005. Originally titled *Our Origin and Destiny: An Evolutionary Perspective of the New Millennium,* A.R.E. Press, 1996. Updated and extensively revised.

In the Image of God and the Shadow of Demons, a Metaphysical Study of Good and Evil, Spirit Song Publications, 2004.

Living in the Spirit, Applying Spiritual Truth in Daily Life, Spirit Song Publications, 2002.

Unseen Hands and Unknown Hearts, A Miracle of Healing Created through Prayer, A.R.E. Press, 1995.

Kathy's books can be purchased at:

www.noble-minds.com

Selected books available at:

www.edgarcayce.org

PREFACE

There are many paths that lead to spiritual enlightenment. The Path of the Medicine Wheel is but one such means that can help you gain a clearer understanding of your true self, your relationships with others, and your relationship to the Creative Spirit.

Medicine Wheel teachings are based in Nature, the world we see around us. The movement of the moons and the flow of the seasons hold meaning for us and can be used to guide our steps. The elements that inhabit Planet Earth such as the rocks, the plants and the animals with which we share this planet, hold lessons for us as well. We need only attune ourselves to the wonder that surrounds us to hear their voices.

This book is a simple yet comprehensive guide to the holistic teachings of the Medicine Wheel. It is based upon a synthesis of teachings drawn from different Native American traditions and includes exercises designed to help you experience the power of the Medicine Wheel in a practical way.

The writing of any book is a labor of love; this tome is no different. We hope it opens the door to a wondrous tool you can use on your own spiritual journey. Allow Spirit to guide you, and may you find what you seek in these pages.

~Kathy L. Callahan
~Deirdre L. Aragon

TABLE OF CONTENTS

Appendix

INTRODUCTION

The Medicine Wheel is an ancient means of using the attributes and creatures of Planet Earth to help us better understand ourselves, our associations with others, and our relationship to our Spiritual Source. It is built upon the sacred circle or *mandala*, which is Sanskrit for circle. The sacred circle dates back to the cave art of Paleolithic times when Cro-Magnon man painted spirals and sun wheels upon cave walls. It appears in Hinduism, Buddhism, Christianity, Gnosticism, Wicca, and other religions. In most religions it is a symbol of introspection and contemplation. In Zen, it is the symbol of enlightenment. In ritual it is frequently used as a means of protection—evil cannot pass through the boundary of the circle.

The Sacred Circle

The sacred circle is a symbol of the *unity* of all that dwell upon the earth. It is also a symbol of *eternity* as it has no beginning and no end. All that exists on the circle is connected and equal. Legend says that King Arthur chose the circle as the design for his famous Round Table because it had no head seat. All the knights that sat at it, including the king, were equals. The circle also represents an endless creation that connects us not only to the present, but also to the ancestors of our past and to a vision of the future.

A wheel was shown to me, wonderful to behold.
Divinity… is like a wheel, a circle, a whole, that can neither be understood,
nor divided, nor begun nor ended… no one has the power
to divide this circle, to surpass it, or to limit it.
~ Hildegard of Bingen

While the Medicine Wheel is identified with Native American cultures, other forms of the sacred circle exist in culture areas around the world, including Africa, India, Siberia, Polynesia, the Middle East, and Europe. Egyptian hieroglyphs of Horus and his four sons, the kivas of the Anasazi, elaborate Celtic spiral designs, the prayer wheels of Buddhism, and the labyrinth designs in medieval cathedrals, all honor the power of the sacred circle.

The great stone circles of Europe such as Stonehenge remain as monuments to the power of the sacred circle. These great circles were built during a time when people valued the harmony of relationships above all else. This included one's relationship with others, with the world around us, with the Creator, and perhaps most importantly, with oneself. They come from a simpler time when humans existed in a state of harmony with their environment. It was a time when Mother Earth was valued for her teachings and the lessons that could be learned simply by observing the web of life as it played out upon the physical plane of this planet.

The value of the sacred circle was introduced to modern western thought by psychiatrist Carl G. Jung, who used the mandala as a tool in the process of individuation. Individuation is the process whereby a person forges the conscious and unconscious minds, thereby achieving a state of full development and completion. Mandalas are used in psychotherapy to help patients identify the disparate parts of their psyche and bring them together into an integrated whole.

When I began drawing the mandalas…I saw that everything,
all the paths I had been following, all the steps I had taken,
were leading back to a single point - namely, to the mid-point.
It became increasingly plain to me that the mandala is the center.
It is the exponent of all paths. It is the path to the center, to individuation…
I began to understand that the goal of psychic development is the self…
I knew that in finding the mandala as an expression of the self
I had attained what was for me the ultimate.
~ Carl Jung

Ancient Medicine Wheels

"Medicine Wheel" is a modern term that has been applied to the remains of over seventy circular stone structures scattered throughout the Plains of North America, two-thirds of which are in Alberta, Canada. The patterns and size vary from a few feet to sixty yards in diameter. The largest cairns—a grouping of piled stones—are twelve feet high and ten yards wide; tons of rocks were used in their construction. Some wheels have spokes extending from the center while others do not. There is little archeological evidence to shed light on the actual use of the Medicine Wheel, though recent studies indicate they were used to track both astronomical phenomena and the passing of the seasons. It is believed that the more recent wheels were built by Plains tribes and used in ceremonies that called forth protective spirits to bring health, fertility, food, and protection to the tribe.

The term Medicine Wheel was first used to describe a large stone circle in Bighorn, Wyoming. The Bighorn Medicine Wheel is located at the 9,642-foot summit of Medicine Mountain. This summit is reachable only during the warm summer months near the time of Summer Solstice. An outer circle of stone eight feet in diameter surrounds a twelve-foot wide and two-foot high central cairn. There are six peripheral cairns, one inside the circle and five outside.

There is evidence that a wooden pole once extended upward from the central cairn. Twenty-eight rays or spokes made of stone travel outward from the central core to the outer circle, making it look much like the wheel of a bicycle. The number twenty-eight may have been a sacred number to the Plains Indians. It is the number of poles used in the roofs of Lakota ceremonial buildings. It also marks the number of days in a lunar cycle.

The Bighorn Medicine Wheel was studied by astronomer John Eddy, who determined that the smaller cairns align with the rising and setting of the Summer Solstice sun, while the others align with the stars Sirius in Canis Major, Aldeberan in Taurus, and Rigel in Orion. These three stars are key stars in the Lakota constellation called the "Animal," and are associated with Summer Solstice. Aldebaran rises two days before Summer Solstice; Rigel rises 28 days after the solstice, while Sirius rises 28 days after that. Another astronomer, Jack Robinson, later identified a cairn pair that aligned with the star Fomalhaut's (Pisces) rising point with the sun 28 days prior to Summer Solstice. The star alignments to the cairns are most accurate for the period of 1,050 to 1,450 C.E.

Perhaps the oldest Medicine Wheel in existence is the Moose Mountain Medicine Wheel in southern Saskatchewan, Canada. Dr. Eddy also studied this wheel and demonstrated that it displays spectacular Summer Solstice alignments to the same stars as the Bighorn Medicine Wheel. The alignments of this wheel are most accurate for the period 200 B.C.E. to 100 C.E. Radiocarbon dating of charcoal found at the bottom of the central cairn dates to 440 B.C.E. This means the tradition of the Medicine Wheel predates Christianity by 500 years! It also indicates that Native American knowledge of the cyclic events of astronomy may have been far more advanced than previously believed.

A modern Medicine Wheel received popular acclaim through the writings of Sun Bear, a Chippewa medicine man, who received his Medicine Wheel in a vision. The Sun Bear Medicine Wheel represents the wheel of life. There is a cross in the center that represent the four directions—North, East, South, and West; the four colors of man—red, black, yellow, and white; and the four seasons—Winter, Spring, Summer, and Autumn. A medicine pouch in the center holds the four sacred medicines—sweet grass, sage, tobacco, and cedar. The teachings of this medicine wheel are balance, harmony, and the brotherhood of all humankind.

"Let the medicine of the sacred circle prevail. Let many people across the land come to the circle and make prayers for the healing of the Earth Mother.

Let the circles of the Medicine Wheel come back."
In this vision were gathered people of all the clans, of all the directions,
of all the totems, and in their hearts they carried peace.
That was the vision I saw.
~Sun Bear

From the Moose Mountain Medicine Wheel to its much younger though more spectacular sister Bighorn, to Sun Bear's vision, Medicine Wheel phenomena span over 2,000 years. We cannot say how the ancient wheels were used in the ritual or ceremonies of Native American cultures. They are cloaked in the mystery of time, and we may never uncover clues to help us truly understand how they were used by the ancients. What we can do, however, is look at the folklore of Native Americans and connect those teachings with how the Medicine Wheel can be used today.

The Medicine Wheel and Shamanism

Some people have the misperception that the path of the Medicine Wheel and shamanism are the same thing. This is not the case. The word "shaman" was first used by anthropologists because of its very specific meaning. It comes from the language of the Tungus tribe of Siberia and refers to a person who travels in an altered state of consciousness to a "nonordinary" reality. This altered state of consciousness was often induced by certain techniques, such as the repetition of a sound (drum beats or a rattle), fasting, or other physically tiring activities such as a sweat lodge or a vision quest. While some tribes used psychedelic drugs to induce this state, such use was ritualized and carefully monitored.

While the teachings of the Medicine Wheel are part of a shaman's way, being a shaman means much more. It is not something you can learn from a book or even by taking a class. You can no more become a shaman by reading about the Medicine Wheel than you can become a priest by reading the Bible. In some traditional cultures shaman are chosen by the spirits; if the spirits don't choose you, there is little you can do to make them accept you as a shaman. In some cultures, shaman is a hereditary position. A shaman was sometimes identified prior to birth while at other times a child—through a near death experience—was clearly chosen by the spirits to follow the shamanic path. While the Medicine Wheel can help you attune to the Creative Spirit, learning the way of the Medicine Wheel does not automatically make you a shaman. The Universe simply does not work that way.

What the Medicine Wheel teachings can do is give us a holistic foundation upon which to base our lives. These teachings show us that there was a time when humans were more closely connected with the forces of Nature and the elements of Mother Earth. They lived in harmony with the animals, observed their ways and understood the lessons they had to share. The plants also held lessons for them; they learned their secrets of power and healing. They respected the wisdom of the rocks, minerals and crystals that have been here since the beginning of time. They listened to the wind and respected the power of thunder and lightning. Grandfather Sun and Grandmother Moon were honored for their life-giving light and illumination. Each season held meaning and marked the passing of yet another step on the continually revolving circle of life, death and rebirth.

The sacred teachings help us learn more about the natural world in which we live, and as we learn more about that world, we discover more about ourselves. As we learn more about our relationship to that world, we better understand our relationships with others. As we learn about the power of that world, we learn how to draw upon that power to help us live more balanced and harmonious lives.

By walking the path of the Medicine Wheel, we open ourselves to spiritual growth of the highest order. As you walk this path you will discover the threads of your past, your present and your future. You will learn how to weave those threads into a beautiful tapestry that reveals from whence you have come, where you now walk, and whither you are going. And so we begin our journey upon the many spirals of the path of the Medicine Wheel.

1

TEACHINGS OF THE MEDICINE WHEEL

The teachings of the Medicine Wheel are diametrically opposed to the teachings of modern Western culture. They cannot be learned from a book or taught in a course. Learning these teachings requires more than an intellectual effort. It requires a willingness to put aside preconceived ideas and open oneself to new ways of seeing, thinking and feeling.

To follow the path of the Medicine Wheel is to embark upon an experiential journey. While you can read the words of the teachings, to truly follow this path you must *experience* the lessons it has to offer. You must absorb the feelings and emotions of each lesson. You must incorporate new perceptions into your being. You must open yourself to change and be willing to become a new person.

As you walk the path of the Medicine Wheel, you must embrace the qualities of each spirit animal. You must feel the wind rush beneath your wings *as* Eagle. You must plunge straightforward through the darkness of the sea *as* Sturgeon. You must run effortlessly and tirelessly *as* Horse. You must be strength *as* Bear. You must become the wisdom that Turtle possesses.

The path of the Medicine Wheel is not quickly mastered. Like any spiritual practice, it takes time and patience to master its teachings. In fact, most teachers will tell you that the path of the Medicine Wheel is a lifelong journey; as we master one lesson, another appears. As we progress through this workbook, I can only present an intellectual understanding of the Medicine Wheel teachings. It is up to you to take this knowledge and begin your experiential journey of self-discovery and attunement. I've included several exercises—guided imagery and meditations—to aid you as you proceed along your path.

There are many traditions of Medicine Wheel teachings associated with a number of Native America tribes such as the Lakota, Ojibwa, and Cheyenne, to name only a few. Differences between these traditions often center around where a specific teaching is placed on the Medicine Wheel. For example, one tradition may place the element Fire in the East while another places it in the South. The teachings presented in this book are not drawn from one specific tradition, but rather reflect a synthesis of different traditions, filtered with a bit of intuition by the author. These teachings can be thought of as an ecumenical or universal interpretation of known teachings.

The major teachings of the Medicine Wheel come from its shape and the placement of various "elements" within the wheel itself. These include the four directions, the elements, the seasons, and the cycles of the day. As we walk the path of the Medicine Wheel we also learn from the plants, minerals, totem clans, moons, and from the spirit animals that walk the path with us. The four major teachings of the Medicine Wheel are: Unity, Balance, Growth/Movement, and Attunement.

Unity

The UNITY teaching comes from the shape of the wheel itself. The circle is a symbol of oneness, completion and eternity. A circle is continuous. When you walk the circle there is nothing that separates you from anyone else on the circle. All are equal. A circle is whole unto itself; there is nothing you can add to make it any more complete. The circle has no beginning, no middle, and no end, and as such it also symbolizes eternity.

In ritual, a circle symbolizes a sacred space that facilitates communication with the spirit world. A circle is purified and consecrated. The space within the circle is safe and protected in that no evil spirits or energy may cross the boundary of the circle. While in the circle, a person may expand his or her consciousness and commune with the unseen forces that surround us. As consciousness is expanded, spiritual growth is achieved.

In Medicine Wheel traditions, the circle represents Mother Earth, or the Sacred Hoop. Our ancestors saw all life as moving in a circular pattern and often equated it with the rhythms of nature. In nature a seed is planted and nourished. It grows, is harvested and is reborn again as a seed, which begins the eternal cycle once more. We too are born, grow and die, only to be reborn again, in our children and grandchildren, or perhaps in another life. The circle is the way of growth and learning. It is the way of life. By entering the sacred circle, we become aware of the web of life that connects all living and nonliving things.

Balance

The teaching of BALANCE comes from the placement of elemental powers around the Medicine Wheel. Fire is balanced with Water, which is balanced with Earth, which is balanced with Air. Water nourishes the Earth while Fire cleanses it. Air gives Fire the power to burn, while Water ensures Fire keeps it place. All four elements exist in a balanced relationship.

Balance also comes from the placement of the seasons and the cycles of the day around the wheel. The dormancy of Winter (Midnight) is followed by the new life of Spring (Sunrise), which is followed by the growth of Summer (Mid-Noon), which is followed by the harvest of Autumn (Sunset). Each season shares its space on the wheel with all others. No one dominates the other; they exist in perfect balance. From the teaching of Balance comes the knowledge of HARMONY, the ability to accept things as they come and to "live and let live" as you move within the ebb and flow of life.

Movement and Growth

As we walk the Medicine Wheel we learn that the world around us is in a constant state of flux. All of nature moves in a cyclic pattern of growth and development. To grow is to be open to all that life has to offer: new knowledge, new teachings and new ways of living. To cease to move is to become stagnant. Stagnation means a loss of connection with the web of life and eventually leads to isolation and death. Only through growth and change do we survive.

As you pass through the various positions on the wheel, you learn about the different directions, seasons, elements, moons, plants, and animals. You experience their strengths and weaknesses. You become open to new ways of thinking, new ways of seeing and new ways of living in the world. As you open yourself to change, you open yourself to a world of unlimited possibilities. You open yourself to the fullness of life.

Attunement

The American Heritage Dictionary of the English Language, Fourth Edition 2000, defines attunement as "a harmonious or responsive relationship." *Roget's II: The New Thesaurus*, Third Edition, 1995, describes it as "a united whole that combines, embodies, and incorporates." Attunement is the state of awareness that comes from knowing who you are and where you belong in the majestic scheme of the Universe. It is remembering your connections to all your relations on Earth.

Attunement comes from the three teachings that precede it and occurs on several levels: physical, emotional, mental, and spiritual. As you learn the lessons of the Medicine Wheel, you discover your true potential as a vital physical being who is connected to all other living things on this planet. You learn to release long buried negative motions that inhibit growth and change. You expand the boundaries of your intellect as you realize the only limits are those you impose upon yourself. You come to understand that you are a valued part of creation, beloved by the Creator, and brought into being for one purpose: to realize your full potential as a child of the Creative Spirit.

Additional teachings come from the "constituents" within the wheel itself. A Medicine Wheel is laid out in alignment with the four cardinal points: North, East, South, and West.

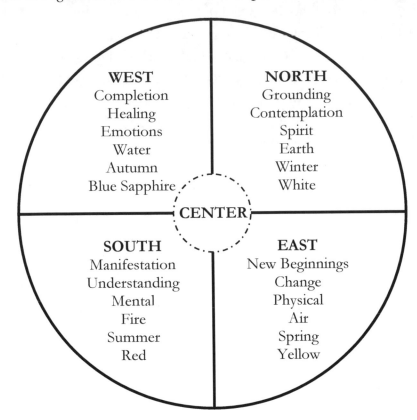

Figure 1. Medicine Wheel Grid

Each direction has a corresponding meaning, element, season, cycle of the day, color, plant, mineral, and totem clan. Each direction also correlates to seasonal moons and their associated spirit animals. As we walk the Medicine Wheel, we learn from the sacred four directions and their correspondences. We also learn lessons from the moons of the Medicine Wheel and the spirit animals that walk the wheel with us. These teachings are discussed in the following chapters. Table 1, *Medicine Wheel Correspondences*, found in the *Appendix*, provides a list of these correspondences for handy reference.

2

THE SACRED FOUR:
NORTH, EAST, SOUTH, AND WEST

A Medicine Wheel is aligned with the four cardinal points of the compass: North, East, South, and West. In effect, this creates four quadrants within the wheel. Four is a sacred number to many indigenous peoples. In addition to the four directions, there are four elements and four seasons marked in the celestial sphere by a solstice or equinox, and four times of the day that also correspond to the phases of our life. There are also four sacred plants, four minerals, and four totem clans. Each directional quadrant contains three seasonal moons and their associated spirit animals.

There are many ways to walk the path of the Medicine Wheel. Some begin in the North while others begin in the East. Most walk the path in a clockwise direction. No particular way is more "right" or better than another; they simply represent a different perspective. The Medicine Wheel that is presented in this book begins in the East and moves in a clockwise manner. I prefer the East as it represents the place of new birth. It is the point where Grandfather Sun rises and gives birth to a new day. Just as Grandfather Sun moves clockwise across the mantle of Mother Earth, we will walk the Medicine Wheel in a clockwise direction. Mother Earth rotates in a clockwise manner and revolves around Grandfather Sun in the same clockwise fashion. In turn, Grandfather Sun revolves clockwise around the center of the Milky Way Galaxy. All of life, even as it extends to the stars, moves in this circular rhythm.

As you walk the Medicine Wheel and pass through each quadrant, you will learn what that direction means in terms of the cycle of life. By becoming aware of the meaning of each direction and its correspondences, you experience different aspects of life and by doing so, attain a new level of awareness and knowing.

The East

We begin our journey in the East. The East is a time of new beginnings and change. It is a time of springing forth with new growth. It can be thought of as the time the first shoot of the planted seed breaks through the womb of Mother Earth and is born into the light. It is a time of outward, visible growth that comes after the dormancy of the cold winter months. The element associated with the North is Air, its season is Spring (Spring Equinox), and its cycle of the day is Sunrise. I see the color of the East as yellow, the color of the rising sun, the dawn of a new day.

When we are born in the East, knowledge comes to consciousness. As we walk in the East we walk in a new world, a world filled with hope and anticipation for things yet to come. Like a toddler learning to walk, we take our first "baby steps," sometimes falling down as we try our hand at new skills. With repeated practice and patience, we find the inner strength to pick ourselves up and move forward unafraid.

The East is the physical quadrant of the wheel, where our physical self comes into being and where we step out into the physical world. Many things will come to us in this new world and there will be many ways we can grow based upon the choices we make. Not all of these paths lead to our highest good, however. We must consider the opportunities that present themselves and choose those that offer us the highest spiritual growth. If we keep our eye toward the wisdom of Grandfather Sun, we will grow straight and true in that direction.

The plant associated with the East is tobacco or kinnick-kinnick, which is actually a tobacco mixture of several plants. There are different mixtures but most include red clover, mullein, bearberry, red willow bark, and sometimes sage and osha root. Kinnick-kinnick was considered a sacred tobacco and was smoked in the medicine pipe during ceremonies to aid communication with the spirits. It was also used during the vision quest. It clears the mind, calms the soul and helps you attune to the energies of the Earth. Through the sacred smoke of kinnick-kinnick you can hear the spirits and bring their wisdom into the physical plane.

The stone associated with the East is amber, a fossilized resin. While it is found in an array of colors such as red, gold, brown, yellow, green, and white, the most common form is a honey-colored stone. Amber helps to release negative energy and bring cleansing and renewal; it was used in the fire ceremonies of ancient healers. It provides an energy that awakens self-realization and the power of choice. By connecting the conscious self to the Universal Mind it helps us make the right choices.

Amber has been used as a symbol of renewal and protection for thousands of years. It was used during wedding ceremonies and to seal alliances. Warriors also carried it into battle as an amulet with protective powers. Meditating with amber as you walk in the East will help you clear out negative energy, empower you to make the right choices and protect you on your journey.

The totem animal of the East is Eagle, the ruler of the Air. Eagle often flies at a height that gives him a 360-degree view of the horizon. He thus sees all of the Earth as it moves below him. Eagle's great strength allows him to fly to Grandfather Sun. He represents power, light, illumination, and vision. He can see a tiny rodent in the bush as he soars hundreds of feet in the sky. Eagle is the link between heaven and earth.

During flight, Eagle swoops, dives and performs dizzying free-falls from fantastic heights. His great vision allows him to do so fearlessly, as he sees all that is in the sky and on the land. While he engages in these magnificent aerial acrobatics, he is always aware of who he is and where he is within the Medicine Wheel landscape. Eagle is vision, power and success. As you become one with Eagle, you see with his vision and move forward with power to manifest your destiny. You will see the totality of the Medicine Wheel landscape and know your place and path within it.

The powers of the East are new beginnings and change. As you walk in the East your physical abilities come forth as you learn and grow. You step forward into a new world of wonder and excitement. You learn to look forward to what lies ahead and to embrace the future with hope and anticipation.

The South

Following our journey in the East, we move to the South. The South is a time of understanding and manifestation. The South is your outer life, the present—what you are doing in the "now." It can be thought of as the time when the young plant that sprouted from the buried seed reaches toward the sky. The roots of the plant have grown deep, its branches are strong, and its leaves and petals grow full as the plant has been nurtured by the warmth of the Sun. The element of the South is Fire, its season is Summer and its cycle of the day is Noon. The color I see in the South is red, the color of fire, of blood, and of life.

Our time in the South is a time of rapid activity and learning. It is a time of looking outward. We see the wonders that surround us and we eagerly explore the many things the world has to offer. We stride forward with confidence in our ability to handle anything that comes our way.

The South represents your mental self, the time when you learn to use your mental abilities to bring ideas into manifestation. As we walk in the South, we feel the full energy and power of the Earth. We revel in our own strength and grow into our power. We take the lessons we have learned thus far and bring them into fulfillment. Our life's purpose comes into focus and we begin to understand our place in the world. We realize our true potential and act to make that potential a reality.

The plant of the South is sweet grass, a tall grass that is native to the prairies and plains of North America. It grows from Alaska to South Carolina; it also grows in Europe. Sweet grass reaches its full growth at the height of the hot summer. Its long blades reach twenty inches in length. The slender blades can be woven into braids and were used in making baskets. Sweet grass braids were also burned as a vanilla-scented incense in ceremonies. This scent is most prominent when the leaves have been dried. The smoke of sweet grass is believed to have cleansing powers and was often used in sacred ceremonies.

Garnet is the stone that corresponds to the South. The color of garnet is a deep red, the color of the South. The garnet has been used as a sacred stone by many Native American tribes including the Mayans and Azetcs. It was held sacred by many African tribes as well. It can awaken a person's internal creative powers and stimulate one's ability to use their powers to bring thought into physical manifestation. Garnet also has healing properties as it extracts negative energy and balances energy fields within the body.

The totem animal of the South is the Mountain Lion, also called Cougar or Puma. Lion represents passion, strength and vitality. She is an animal of great physical power. Lion lives in the world with great passion and strength; she teaches you to look outward and to accept the truth of the world as it is. Lion moves with elegance and grace; she teaches you to be comfortable with your body's powers. Lion is a social animal, always surrounded by the pride. She teaches you to draw strength from your family and community.

Lion fears nothing and moves through the world with purpose and courage. When Lion spots prey, she does not hesitate but rather seizes the moment with confidence and strength. When Lion walks beside you, you are protected and strong. You are empowered to act. Lion is power in manifestation.

The powers of the South are manifestation and understanding. A journey in the South teaches you to focus your thoughts and dreams and bring them into physical reality. You come to understand the power you possess and learn how to manifest that power in ways that will make your dreams come true in the physical world.

The West

We continue our journey as we move to the West. The West is a time of healing and completion. The plant that began as the seed buried beneath the snows of the North, was nurtured by the sun of the East, and grew strong in the South, is now ready for harvest. The element associated with the West is Water, the season is Autumn and the cycle of the day is Sunset. While many see the color of the West as black, I see it as blue, a deep sapphire blue, and the third of the primary colors. It is a hue that merges the blues of the twilight sky with the black of night.

In the West we have the setting sun, the gradual change from daylight to darkness. As you walk in the West, you are fulfilled and complete. You are the sum of what you have experienced and the lessons you have lived. Yet you are more than that, for the true lesson of the West is that you are not defined by the experiences of life, but by how you responded to those experiences. This is the lesson of wisdom—the realization that your life is what you have made of it.

The West represents the maturing of our emotional self. It is through the balancing of our emotions that healing will come. When you walk in the West of the Medicine Wheel, you walk in peace and power, a power that comes from an inner strength of knowing who you are. You reflect and look back upon your life, keeping the good and releasing the bad. Through this self-reflection and evaluation, you are healed and made whole. You gather the power of spirit within yourself and prepare for the renewal that is to come as you pass out of the West and into the northern night of introspection.

Sage, the plant of the West, is perhaps the most sacred of all plants. The many varieties of sage are known throughout the world for their great healing properties. It is classified as an aromatic, antihydrotic, antispasmodic, and astringent. It does reduce excessive perspiration in the body and therefore cleanses the body of toxins. Sage can be chewed, ingested, smoked, or made into a tea. When prepared as a tea, it is taken to cure colds, flu and fever. Native Americans burned dried sage in the smudging ceremony, a sacred ritual of cleansing and purification. The smoke is believed to cleanse the space in which it is burned, bringing healing to the people and animals who reside there.

The stone of the West is turquoise, one of the great healing stones. Blue turquoise brings clarity and tranquility to its wearer. Like sage, its energy purifies and cleanses, refreshing the body and soul like a gentle swim in a cool mountain stream. Turquoise heals by bringing the blue of Father Sky to Mother Earth and blending these energies into one. It therefore both heals the body and brings about spiritual attunement. A protective stone, it will also guide you through the unknown.

Bear is the totem animal of the West, the chief of the council of animals. When Bear is threatened, he stands on two legs, like Man, and moves forward to meet the danger head on. The lesson here is to face our problems rather than run from them. This lesson does not come from physical strength, however, but from inner strength, the ability to look within and know that you possess everything you need to succeed in life. Bear's position as chief does not come from his great physical prowess but from this inner spiritual strength, for Bear has looked into his own heart and knows what lies there. From this inner knowing comes Bear's ability to look into the hearts of others and by doing so, help them see the lessons they need to learn.

When Bear eats he uproots many plants. In the old medicine ways, roots have great healing powers. This may be why Bear is often called Medicine Bear, for he has the ability to heal himself. Bear's greatest power, however, comes from his ability to heal others by helping them look within and understand the power that lies within them. Bear goes through solitary periods of hibernation. It is during this time that he enters the spirit world and learns how to create and hold sacred space. Bear is thus a powerful shaman in his own right.

The powers of the West are completion and healing. You are complete in that you have experienced all that life has to offer. Your emotions are in balance and you are healed by the wisdom that you have created your life as you walked this path. By walking in the West, you understand that the power you once thought lay outside you, truly lies within you. You are now ready to enter the final quadrant of the Medicine Wheel—the mysterious North.

The North

The North is a time of grounding and contemplation. It is a time of introspection, hidden growth and inner change. The North is a place of duality. It is the time of the elders—the crone, the wise woman, the wizard, and the sage. Yet it is also the time of preparation for new life. It can be thought of as the time a newly planted seed lies beneath the ground. From the surface, it appears the seed is dormant and inactive, yet the seed is experiencing internal change, taking in the nutrients that it will need later as it pushes its roots deeper into the ground and sends its first shoot to break through the womb of Mother Earth and into the open Air. The element associated with the North is Earth, its season is Winter, and its cycle of the day is Midnight. I see the color of the North as white, the color of reflection, clarity and renewal. White is the sum of all colors.

When we walk in the North we rest in the womb of Mother Earth, much like the unborn child rests and forms in the womb of its mother. We take time to rest, to breath deeply and to look within ourselves rather than without. You still the mind and its concerns about the world and focus instead upon yourself, reflecting upon where you have been and what you have learned. You prepare to pass that knowledge on to others.

The North is the time of our spiritual self. It is where our dreams live. The knowledge and wisdom of the old crone and wise sage are internalized as you reflect upon all that has gone before. You determine what things you now hold that no longer serve you and set them aside. You come to understand strengths that lie deep within you, untapped yet ready to come forth. You meditate, reflect, and meditate yet again. As you do this, you become firm in your grounding and draw strength from all the lessons you have learned, even those that caused you pain. This grounding is necessary to ensure a firm foundation is in place to support the new growth and change that will come as you move forward upon your next turn around the path of the Medicine Wheel.

The plant of the North is cedar. Cedar comes in many different forms and in common terms refers to plants of several species, such as the great Cedars of Lebanon, the white cedar of North America, the small red cedar shrubs of New Mexico, and the ancient cedar tress of Japan. The cedar tree sustains life. It provides shelter from the Sun and a safe haven for the homes of many animals and birds. Cedar wood is strong and resistant to temperature, humidity and decay, making it excellent for use in buildings. The Cedars of Lebanon grow eighty feet tall and were used in the construction of the Temple of Solomon and the tombs of Egyptian pharaohs.

Cedar trees are believed to possess healing powers. A tea is made from their needle-like leaves while healing oils and incense are made from their fragrant wood. They also represent survival, as they are some of the oldest plants on earth. The Jomon Cedar of Yakusugi, Japan is estimated to be 2,200 years old. The lessons we learn from cedar are strength, permanence and wholeness.

Clear quartz crystal is the stone of the North. The clear quartz crystal is known for its ability to focus, store, transfer, and transform energy. Clear quartz can amplify both thoughts and energy (for thought is energy) and provide clarity in thinking. Many believe quartz can bring the energy of the stars into the human soul. In ancient teachings, the quartz crystal is believed to possess the ability to harmonize and align human energy with the energies of the Universe.

Clear quartz is recognized as a stone of great power that offers many benefits. It stimulates psychic abilities, activates the energy centers (chakras) of the body, clears emotional disturbance, eliminates negative energies, and brings wisdom and clarity to dreams when placed near the body during sleep. Clear quartz is used extensively in meditation and healing ceremonies. Its energies have been recognized by cultures and religions throughout the world.

The totem animal of the North is Buffalo. Buffalo is considered the true Earth mother. Buffalo does not hunt other animals but rather gives of herself to feed, clothe and provide us with shelter. Her meat provided food, her fur provided clothing and her hide provided material for the teepee. The Buffalo gives her life so others may live.

Buffalo also represents community and the continuity of life. When threatened, the herd places its young in a circle and then surrounds that circle. The elders offer their lives to protect the young and ensure survival of the herd. Buffalo teaches how Mother Earth provides for us. She also teaches us to give of ourselves for the survival of the greater community good.

The powers of the North are grounding, contemplation, self-reflection, and internal growth. As we journey through the North we gain the wisdom and understanding that old age brings. We achieve attunement and balance. We look deep within ourselves and by knowing who we are, we strengthen our connection with the world around us. We grow our roots and form a firm foundation upon which future growth can stand.

The Center

In addition to the sacred four directions of the Medicine Wheel, most traditions also honor the Center, the point from which the directions radiate. While the teachings of the

Medicine Wheel are anchored by the sacred four directions, the directions themselves are anchored by the Center. The Center represents the Creator and is the point at which we meet with the Great Spirit. When we are in the presence of the Creator, we realize we are never alone, for we understand that the Great Spirit also lies within us.

Petrified wood is the stone of the Center. Petrified wood is a type of fossil wood in which all the organic materials have been replaced with minerals (most often a silicate, such as quartz); yet it retains the original structure of the wood. The petrification process occurs underground as water flows through sediment and deposits minerals such as iron, copper and manganese in the plant's cells. As the plant's cellulose decays, a stone cast forms in its place. It is found in many colors including black, red, green, blue, and gray. Petrified wood is honored for its connection with both the plant and mineral worlds. It is used to sustain long life and to restore strength to the body, mind and spirit.

The plant of the Center is the oak tree. The oak tree has long been used as a symbol of strength, wisdom, endurance, and the continuity of life, The name of the Druids, the ancient Celtic priests, stems from the Gaelic words for oak and knowledge. In many legends, the tree which stands at the center of the world is portrayed as a giant oak. A well-known proverb states that the mightiest oak grows from the tiniest acorn, a reference to the ever-changing and transformative nature of life.

The Center is synonymous with Turtle. Native American creation myths say that Turtle emerged from the sea with Mother Earth on her back and provided the place upon which all creatures could live. This is why some people refer to Earth as "Turtle Island." Turtle is thus connected with the creation of the Earth itself. Turtle has existed on Earth since the time of the dinosaur—yet Turtle is still here. Turtle is also the link with those who live in another dimension of time and space.

While Turtle can communicate across different dimensions, she also has a strong sense of self-identity. Turtle lives hundreds of years; she is well grounded, self-sufficient, and protected within the shell she carries. Turtle moves by slowing but deliberately planting each foot upon the ground; she moves with slow but deliberate *intent*. Turtle is tenacious and will not be deterred from her path. She also knows that peace and harmony come from a gentle slowness. This gentle slowness is the heart of meditation—the means by which we too can communicate across the dimensions of time and space and visit the spirit world.

The Center represents the essential or soul-self of every human, ever changing and transforming, moving beyond the seasons of this world and through time itself until we become one with the Creative Spirit.

You begin and end each journey upon the Medicine Wheel in the Center. As you complete your journey through East, North, South, and West, you return to the Center and prepare to begin yet again. For your last step is but the first step of yet another cycle upon the spiral path of the Medicine Wheel.

3

THIRTEEN MOONS

The teachings of the sacred four directions and their correspondences that we learned of in the last chapter are tied to the Sun or solar structure of the web of life. There are other teachings of the Medicine Wheel however, that are tied to the Moon and the lunar cycle. Grandmother Moon is inviting, mysterious and powerful. She controls the tides of the seas, illuminates our way at night and possesses the power to darken the light of the Sun.

On the day of the new moon, in the month of Hiyar,
the Sun was put to shame, and went down in the daytime, with Mars in attendance.
(One of the earliest written records of an eclipse of the Sun by the Moon)
~3 May 1375 BCE, Ugarit, Mesopotamia

Many ancient cultures marked time by the lunar cycle. The phases of the moon provided a consistent and easily observable means of counting time. The Hebrew, Chinese, Hindu, and Islamic calendars are only some of those that are lunar-based. Lunar calendars differ in terms of which day is considered the first day of the month. Some use the day upon which the new moon first arrives while others are based on the first sighting of the lunar crescent. References to time keeping by the lunar cycle still exist in modern times. An example is the word "fortnight" which means two weeks. It comes from the Old English *feowertiene niht*, which literally means "fourteen nights," and is the interval between the full moon and the new moon.

Moon teachings are fluid in that they wax (grow) and wane (diminish) in relation to the movement of the moon's twenty-eight day lunar cycle. The teachings of any particular moon are weakest at the new moon and strongest during the full moon. A new moon therefore is still influenced by the power of the previous moon.

The moon under which you were born is your natal moon. It reflects certain *tendencies* that are part of your personality. It will also give you guidance as to your inner strengths and your potential weaknesses. It may also provide a clue as to your soul's purpose—the primary reason for which you entered the Earth plane. Keep in mind however, that the guiding influences of each moon are just that—influences that you can use for good or ill. No celestial or earthly influence can overcome the individual human will. It is your will that determines the choices you make and the actions you take. You determine who you are.

The current moon is called the calendar moon. As we pass through a calendar moon it is easier to learn the lessons it has to offer. For example, the New Buds Moon of the East can help us find the initiative to start a new project while the Hunters Moon of the West can help us bring a project to conclusion. During the winter moons of the North we find it easier to slow down and spend more time in self-reflection while the summer moons of the South encourage heightened activity.

In this chapter we will learn of the thirteen moons of the Medicine Wheel as well as the plants, stones and spirit animals that are associated with each moon. Table 2, *Moons of the Medicine Wheel*, found in the *Appendix*, outlines the moons and their correspondences.

Moons of the East

The East is the time of new beginnings and change, the time of new growth. In the East we learn about hope. We learn to look forward and know we can become something greater than we are. The three moons of the East begin with the moon of the Vernal or Spring Equinox. At the time of an equinox, the Sun is directly overhead the equator and at that moment both the North Pole and South Pole of Mother Earth are on the terminator (the line dividing the day and night sides of the planet). Therefore day and night are equal and last for twelve hours each across the entire Earth. The moons of the East are:

> ➢ **New Buds Moon** (21 March – 19 April)
> ➢ **Planting Moon** (20 April – 20 May)
> ➢ **New Flowers Moon** (21 May – 20 June)

New Buds Moon. This moon represents the dawn of new life on Mother Earth. The Earth begins to awaken after a Winter of rest and renewal. The hard freezes and cold nights are ending. As the snow melts, the seeds that have been lying dormant beneath the ground will send forth their first shoots. The days gradually become longer and the light of the Sun will warm and nourish the new buds that have sprouted. The animal world comes to life as well. Those that hibernate awaken, eggs are laid and preparations are made for the young animals that are soon to be born.

Red clover—one of the first spring plants to come into bloom—is the plant of New Buds Moon. This plant is a primary food source for many animals as they awaken in the Spring. It is a cleansing plant that can rebuild any part of the body. Its blossoms are used medicinally in a variety of ways including a tonic for respiratory problems, as a poultice to treat cuts and burns, and as a tea with renewal and sedative properties.

Fire opal is the stone of New Buds Moon. The opal has long been a symbol of hope. It draws its power from the Sun, the Moon and from Fire. It possesses great energy and teaches us how to harness the power of the life force. Opal is used to counteract stagnation and helps us visualize new realms of existence. It helps us step out into a new world.

The spirit animal of New Buds Moon is Hawk. Many native peoples consider Hawk a most sacred animal. The Pueblo Indians thought Red Hawk to be a red eagle and believed he had a special connection with the heavens. Their feathers were often used in ceremonies to carry prayers to Grandfather Sun; they were also used in healing ceremonies. Unlike Eagle, Hawk does not fly for the joy of it, but rather flies out of necessity. Hawk spends much time sitting on a perch, watching with clear vision and far-sightedness until he sees a reason to move. When Hawk spots his prey however, he flies forth with intent and great power. Hawk is adaptable and lives in many areas throughout the world. The lessons of Hawk are foresight, deliberation and intent.

People born under New Buds Moon will always possess a sense of innocence and wonder that they carry throughout their lives. Their talent is to recognize the value of new ideas and projects and attempt to bring them into being. Their potential weakness is failure to bring those tasks to completion, as they are often distracted by another new idea and race off to begin a new project before finishing the task at hand. They are most compatible with Hunters Moon people who will help them learn how to complete their efforts. Together they can learn the balance between beginning and completion.

Planting Moon. Planting moon is a time of preparation and renewed activity. It is the time we till and hoe the soil so it can take the seeds we plant, seeds that will provide us with food throughout the coming year. It is the time when most young animals are born, protected and nourished by their parents. Eggs hatch and the baby bird takes in nourishment as it grows within the safety of its nest.

The dandelion is the plant of this moon. Its bright yellow flowers open from dawn to dusk and its leaves and roots provide food and medicine at a time when other vegetation has not yet begun to grow. Its root is a good coffee substitute and its new leaves are used in salads while older leaves make a tasty cooked green. The dandelion can purify and alkalize the blood and help balance blood sugar levels.

The mineral of Planting Moon is citrine. Citrine strengthens your willpower and helps you achieve your goals.   It is a variety of quartz ranging in color from yellow to golden brown to burnt amber. This stone cannot hold negative energy but rather dissipates and transforms it. It stabilizes the emotions, enhances energy, dispels fear, and stimulates mental focus. It encourages you to "look toward the sunrise" for the promise of new beginnings.

The spirit animal of Planting Moon is Beaver, one of the most industrious of all the animals. Beaver represents the harmony of the ebb and flow of life. Beaver teaches us respect for balance, tradition, commitment, and productivity. Beaver moves with deliberate purpose, building great dams one tree at a time. By building a dam, they can change the course of a river or cause a lake to form. The activity of Beaver can change the world. The lesson of Beaver is the mastery of the flow of the life force.

Planting Moon people thrive on hard work and will put enormous effort into any project they undertake. They understand the need for preparation and excel at promoting new ideas. Their potential weakness is an inability to prioritize or choose what needs to be done first. Once they embrace a specific task, however, they give it 110% of their time and effort. Planting Moon people are most compatible with First Freeze Moon people, who can teach them the right seeds to plant. Together they learn the need for taking action and following through with industry and continued effort.

New Flowers Moon. The time of New Flowers Moon is when flowers first blossom and the time fruit and nut trees come into bloom. Young animals begin to explore the world around them and birds whose wings have grown strong learn to fly. It is the time of learning about the world around you and standing on one's own feet.

The apple blossom is the plant of New Flowers Moon. The apple tree is strongest at this time of the year as it sends forth its life force into the blossoms that will grow and mature into fruit that provides the sustenance of life. This blossom, as well as those of the cherry and peach trees, and the pecan and hazel, remind us that the harvest will come later in the year if we tend and nourish the trees.

Coral is the mineral of this moon. This "stone" of the sea is considered a stone of fertility. It also helps balance energy and calm the emotions as it possesses a "negative" ion. It can assist you in attuning to the world's creative forces. In addition to the well-known colors of red, pink and orange, coral is also found in black and white varieties. Coral symbolizes vitality and the balanced energy of life.

Deer is the spirit animal of New Flowers Moon. Deer is alert and sensitive to even the minutest changes in its environment. Deer symbolizes beauty, agility and grace. Deer is the manifestation of beauty and prosperity. She is an omen of good fortune. While Deer may seem timid, she possesses the power of great growth and strength. Deer is heart energy manifested. In some native cultures, such as the Huichol, Deer is the gatekeeper of the spirit world. They have been observed running in spirals of ecstasy around places of power. Deer can bring spirals of beauty and power into your life. The lessons of Deer are beauty, grace and love.

New Flowers Moon people possess a bubbly type of exuberance and enthusiasm. They always seem to be in bloom. They are creative in nature and drawn to artistic endeavors. They make excellent craftsmen or artists. Their potential weakness is the lack of staying power and commitment, and an inability to pay attention to important details. They are most compatible with Silent Snow Moon people who can teach them to think before speaking and share with them the wisdom of knowing when to act and when to wait. New Flowers Moon people need to learn how to keep their joyful character while taking time to devote proper care and consideration to the task at hand.

Moons of the South

The South is a time of manifestation and understanding. In the South we learn to embrace life and enjoy the fullness of the day. We learn to grown, to love and to live fully. This is the time of the June Solstice, when Grandfather Sun is at its greatest distance from Earth's equator. This creates the longest day in the northern hemisphere (Summer Solstice) and the shortest day in the southern hemisphere (Winter Solstice). For our purposes, the South is the time of the June Summer Solstice, and its moons are:

> **Hot Sun Moon** (21 June – 22 July)
> **Hot Winds Moon** (23 July – 22 August)
> **Harvest Moon** (23 August – 22 September)

Hot Sun Moon. Summer Solstice is the strongest day for Grandfather Sun. It is a time of ceremony and rejoicing. It is the time of the first warmth, when the world shines forth in beauty and joy. Plants thrive and grow strong; roots grow deep and leaves mature. Flowers bask in the warmth of the sun. The young grow and leave the shadow of their parents' protection; birds leave their nests. Hot Sun Moon is the time of the child at play.

The wild rose is the plant of Hot Sun Moon. This is not the domesticated, long-stem, American Beauty rose, but the Rugosa rose, a dense shrub rose with short, straight thorns whose leaves have a distinct corrugated pattern. The flowers are pleasantly scented and can be red, lavender, dark pink, or white. They flower from June to September. The hips are large, 2-3 centimeters in diameter and exceptionally bright, with red or orange color. They ripen throughout the summer and are often retained into autumn and winter. Although the Rugosa rose originated in Japan, it was brought to America generations ago. Hardy and resistant to drought and disease, it long ago escaped cultivation and spread out playfully across the countryside.

The mineral of Hot Sun Moon is rose quartz, the stone of the heart. It is known for its healing and calming properties. It brings healing to emotional wounds as it encourages emotional release, understanding, and promotes renewal. Rose quartz can teach you about unconditional love. It is an excellent stone to use with children because it helps one bring forth feelings of love for self. When used by Hot Sun Moon people it will restore balance and calm to their frequently flaming emotions.

The playful Otter is the animal of Hot Sun Moon. Otter enjoys everything he does and he does it with passion. Otter spends most of his time eating, playing, sunning, and raising the young; they are extremely responsible and devoted parents. Otter is family-oriented and has an exemplary home life. Otter is curious and inventive—he learned long ago to use rocks to crack open shellfish. Otter medicine is considered very powerful and was often not taught until a shaman reached a certain degree of learning. The lesson of Otter is living with passion.

Hot Sun Moon people are blessed with a joy for life. They have a playful nature and can brighten up even the dullest day. They are often successful in the area of customer service. A potential weakness is that they are childish in nature and do not understand what the consequences of their actions may be. They are best when paired with Winter moon people, particularly Contemplation Moon people, for they can guide them in setting the best direction to meet their needs.

Hot Winds Moon. Hot Winds Moon is the hottest month of the Medicine Wheel. It is the time when all is ripening or growing into maturity; the hot winds are needed to bring many seeds to ripeness. The heat at this time of year is such that it dries up water sources. Plants and animals must reach deep within their own resources to survive the heat of this moon.

The red raspberry is the plant of Hot Winds Moon. Its berries are considered a delicacy and its leaves have medicinal properties that cleanse the system and break up gallstones and kidney stones. The root has antibiotic properties. Raspberry leaf tea is used as a tonic for female problems while a tea from the twigs can cure respiratory illness. The raspberry plant teaches you to find the sweet fruit within the thorns of life.

The mineral of Hot Winds Moon is carnelian, which is an orange-red colored agate. Carnelian is associated with the heart and emotional healing. The fire of carnelian gives you courage and stability. It creates an emotional balance in the person who wears it and boosts one's energy. It offers protection in that it prevents other people from reading your thoughts. It helps you move forward to the next step on your spiritual path.

Sturgeon is the animal spirit of Hot Winds Moon. Sturgeon is an ancient fish that first appeared around the time the dinosaurs became extinct. Sturgeon is known as the king of the fishes; he can reach twelve feet in length and weighs some 300 pounds. Sturgeon is protected by rows of bony plates, although they do not completely cover his body. Sturgeon was hunted extensively for its roe—caviar—and came near to the brink of extinction. Sturgeon is known for his bravery, strength, noble character, and longevity. The lesson of Sturgeon is perseverance, strength and survival.

People of Hot Winds Moon are the doers of the Medicine Wheel. They will literally go where angels fear to tread. They are versatile and fit into many different places. They may have a certain hardness for they have a tendency to be tempered by the experiences of life. They possess the ability to look within and find the answers they need. They make powerful and loyal friends, yet they also make fierce enemies. A potential weakness of Hot Winds Moon people is taking on too many causes and giving up before they have finished the first. Conversely, they sometimes do not let go when it is wise to do so. They need to guard against stubbornness, arrogance and an air of superiority. They are most compatible with Deep Snow Moon people who can teach them to balance activity with peaceful contemplation and action with rest.

Harvest Moon. Harvest Moon represents the ending of Summer and the beginning of the harvest. It represents the ending of play and the beginning of movement into the full maturity of adulthood. The days begin to shorten and we move toward a time of balance and equality when the days and nights will once again be of equal length. The Sun's dominance is beginning to fade and the power of the night—and the Moon—grows stronger.

The sunflower is the plant of Harvest Moon. This plant, with its bright yellow petals, resembles Grandfather Sun, and therefore bears his name. Their connection to Grandfather Sun is strong, as seen by the way in which they face the direction of Grandfather Sun from sunrise to sunset. Sunflowers represent strength and growth. They can easily reach fourteen feet in height. Their roots grow deep into the earth to support this growth. The seeds, which cluster in the middle of the petals, provide a bounty of food at the time of harvest. The seeds are filled with vitamins and nutrients that promote good health in the kidneys and bladder as well as the heart, skin and teeth. Sunflower oil is used in cooking and in health care products.

Fluorite, the stone of Harvest Moon, is a member of the crystal family and comes in a rainbow of colors: white, purple, blue, violet, green, yellow, red-pink, brown, white, black, and even fluorescent. Fluorite melts with great ease and is therefore used as a flux in the smelting of minerals. By its ability to change and meld with other minerals, fluorite possesses the ability to become something more than itself—that is the lesson it holds for us. Fluorite will give you a new perspective as it helps you integrate information. It promotes balance, expansion and universal unity. It relieves stagnation and can aid in healing. Fluorite helps you grow beyond current limitations and become more than you now are.

The spirit animal of Harvest Moon is Spider, often known as Grandmother Spider in the myths of the Pueblo Indians. Spider knows the symmetry of the web of life. The strands that build her web come from deep inside her and flow outward into beautiful geometric patterns that spiral into infinity. Spider is resourceful, patient and trusting. She builds her web and waits for her prey to come to her, knowing that the Universe will provide what she needs. If her web is destroyed, she immediately begins to weave another. If you are blessed by Spider, you have the ability to affect the web of life and reach out and inspire others. Spider teaches us the lesson of the interconnectedness of all life.

People born under Harvest Moon usually show good judgment, justice and courage when dealing with the realities of life. They possess keen analytical skills and are known for their fairness. They search for the "middle way" and avoid extremes in all things. They have the ability to protect friends and loved ones from falling victim to extremes simply by using their own common sense. While Harvest Moon people are practical and down to earth, they also have the ability to reach forward to the things of the spirit. When they are in balance with themselves and in tune with Mother Earth, they can perceive the truths of the spirit and use their strength to help others achieve spiritual attunement. Harvest Moon people can sometimes be overcome by their sense of the practical and look to apply mystic powers for practical means, resulting in a misuse of power for personal gain. They are most compatible with Strong Winds Moon people, who help keep them grounded and centered.

Moons of the West

The West is the time of healing and completion, a time of maturity and the insight that time brings. In the West we complete our work on the physical plane and begin healing on the emotional level. We begin to look deep within ourselves and learn from the images of our inner thoughts and dreams. By doing so, we take the first steps toward understanding our own healing power. It is the time of the Autumnal or Fall Equinox when day and night are again equal in length. The moons of the West are:

> ➤ **Hunters Moon** (23 September – 23 October)
> ➤ **First Freeze Moon** (24 October – 21 November)
> ➤ **Silent Snow Moon** (22 November – 21 December)

Hunters Moon. The Hunters Moon begins with the Autumnal Equinox when day and night are once again in balance. The animals begin their preparations for the Winter which is to come. The warmth of Grandfather Sun gives way to the coolness of Grandmother Moon and her starry nights. We catch our breath after the hectic growth of the Summer and look forward to the peace and repose that lie ahead.

Bearberry is the plant of Hunters Moon. The bearberry plant is used in kinnick-kinnick, the sacred tobacco. It is a large bush that produces very tart berries that reach their full maturity in early Autumn. The berries have excellent medicinal properties. Bearberry is used to make a tea that is especially good for breaking a fever and relieving stomach upsets.

The stone of Hunters Moon is jasper, a stone believed to bring many blessings. Jasper comes in an array of colors including black, brown, red, blue, yellow, and green. It helps a person to harmonize with Mother Earth's energy by providing a positive and grounding force. Jasper can also help stimulate and clear mental thought and therefore help you find balance in the physical world. It is reported to be able to stop bleeding and draw poison from a snakebite. It also has protective properties.

Wolf is the spirit animal of Hunters Moon. Wolf is a teacher and pathfinder. She will help you find your way through the complexities of your inner self. Wolf knows the secrets held by Grandmother Moon—hence why she communicates (howls) with her each evening. Wolf is strong-willed and individual yet lives in a very complex social structure. Wolves work together to ensure the survival of the pack; they work as a team to bring down large animals. Wolf is loyal and puts the welfare of the pack above her own. Wolf understands the need to work with others and can therefore help you understand the dynamics of relationships. Wolf teaches us to recognize our personal power and the strength of power that comes from the collective consciousness.

Like Wolf, people of Hunters Moon are kind, loving, considerate, and truly concerned with the welfare of others. They are openhearted and will generously listen to another's problems and offer solutions. They are happiest in a group that shares their own ideals. Autumn is when Mother Earth slows down her previous frenetic growth. Hunters Moon people need to learn this lesson, for by slowing themselves down, they can reach a point of balance. When balanced, they possess the ability to unite the powers of Mother Earth with the power of spirit. If they do not attain this balance, however, they have a tendency to be ruled by their emotions and fly from one mood to another.

First Freeze Moon. First Freeze Moon is the moon during which the first snowfall occurs. Morning frosts are common and the nights grow cold. Plants that grew strong in the warmth of Grandfather Sun now wither and die. The leaves fall from trees and only their roots remain alive beneath the ground. Animal and plant life prepares for the oncoming sleep that comes with the Winter.

Mullein is the plant associated with First Freeze Moon. This is one plant that survives well into the moons of the West. It is a tall plant growing six feet in height with velvet leaves and a tall spike of flowers in various shades of yellow, pink, red, and purple. Mullein possesses great healing properties. Used as a tea, mullein soothes mucous membranes and heals the lungs, heart, kidneys, bladder, and liver. It can be used as an astringent and when applied externally will heal sores, ulcers and even muscle injuries. Oil made from mullein flowers is used as eardrops. Its leaves can also be smoked to help relieve bronchitis and lung congestion.

The stone of First Freeze Moon is malachite. Malachite is a copper carbonate, always green in color with dark striations running through it. Malachite has the ability to awaken a person's sensitivity to the voice of spirit. It therefore helps you to develop psychic abilities. It is a stone that facilitates change and helps people understand their developing connection with the world of spirit.

Owl is the spirit animal of First Freeze Moon. Owl is diurnal—an animal that is most active at twilight. You can most easily observe their activity during the Autumn following the Equinox. While Owl has large eyes that help it see well at night, she also has very acute hearing. Her forward-placed ears and the dish-shaped feathers that surround them draw in sound. Owl is wise and is thought to be a messenger of the old wisdom and knowledge that carries the power of the feminine. Owl medicine is thus very powerful, dating back to the earliest times of shamanism in Siberia. Owl will teach you to look deep within yourself to see who you truly are. Owl also sees through the veil of death to the other side. The lesson Owl gives us is that of inner vision.

First Freeze Moon people are much like Owl. They can seem mysterious and secretive, and it takes a long time for them to open up to others. Yet once they come to know you, they are warm and giving. They have the ability to see into the depths of the soul, both their own and other's. They are patient and cautious yet do not hesitate to take action when they can see the end result in sight. First Freeze Moon people understand the value of feminine power—the power of insight that the night brings.

Silent Snow Moon. Silent Snow Moon marks the transition from the moons of the West to the Winter moons of the North. Both days and nights are cold and the silence that accompanies a snowfall begins to settle upon the Earth. The animals make their last preparations for the Winter slumber that will soon enfold Mother Earth. The stars sparkle most brightly at this time of the year, and we are drawn to the beauty of the night Sky. We begin to wonder about our connection with the greater Universe.

The birch tree is the plant of Silent Snow Moon. Birch bark and its leaves were used for medicinal purposes, to help expel toxins, treat skin conditions and aid in digestive problems. Branches of birch were bound together and used to help cleanse the body during sweat lodge ceremonies. Used in this way, birch was thought to bring knowledge of ancient wisdom to the person seeking a vision. Birch opens up your energies and cleanses you so you may attune to the powers of the Universe.

The stone of Silent Snow Moon is hematite. Hematite is ferric oxide, a part of iron ore. Its color ranges from steel gray to metallic silver to black; there are even red forms. This is a recorder stone, meaning that it can be programmed to hold a memory across the eons of time. It has the ability to share these memories with those who know how to access its knowledge. It can therefore help you learn from the lessons of the past so you will not repeat the same mistakes.

Horse is the spirit animal of Silent Snow Moon. A companion to humans, Horse teaches us about relationships and how to honor the power of others without losing ourselves. Horse also represents strength and movement. Horse is the vehicle that takes you into the spirit world. As the spirit animal of the last moon of the West, Horse will transport you to the spirit moons of the North. Horse represents relationships, prosperity and also embodies work that needs to be done. Horse can withstand pain and injustice and bear these things with great dignity. Horse helps us travel between Earth and the spirit world and teaches us to do work in both. Horse will take you to your deepest love. The lesson of Horse is knowledge of travel between the worlds.

Silent Snow Moon people are often strong of body and will. They possess an inner strength that helps them know the right direction to follow and also helps them lead others to the right path. As children of Silent Snow Moon, the time when all Earth's children prepare for the Winter season of renewal, they are blessed with the ability to understand and use the thoughts of spirit that flow through them. Intuitive to their own feelings as well as those of others, they can help others release resentments they are holding. They know that the answers lie within and not without, and can help others achieve this understanding. They make excellent teachers.

Moons of the North

The North is the time of contemplation and grounding. In the North we learn to go deep within ourselves to find our connection with the Universe. We come to understand our dreams and work to turn them into reality. We build our spiritual foundation—our cornerstone—during our time in the North. It is the time of the December Solstice, which creates the longest day in the southern hemisphere (Summer Solstice) and the shortest day in the northern hemisphere (Winter Solstice). The moons of the North are:

> **Contemplation Moon** (22 December – 19 January)
> **Deep Snow Moon** (20 January – 18 February)
> **Strong Winds Moon** (19 February – 20 March)

Contemplation Moon. The Winter Solstice marks the beginning of our time in the North, a time of rest and renewal for the greater journey of rebirth that yet lies ahead. It is the time when we turn our sight within, connect with Creative Spirit and learn to bring forth the power of our spiritual self. Contemplation Moon is the first moon of this quiet time of introspection.

The plant of Contemplation Moon is chamomile. It has long been known as the plant of introspection. Chamomile tea can help you achieve a deep level of relaxation that takes you to a point where you can look deep within your own being. It is used as a healer of both bodily and spiritual pain. As a preventive medicine, it was used as a staple of childhood diets to prevent later heath problems. It is used to cure colds, flu, measles, mumps, earaches, and headaches. It eases heavy menstrual bleeding. Used as an oil or salve it is good for treating skin irritations.

Lapis lazuli, the stone of Contemplation Moon, is the stone of introspection. It has a blue tint with hues of royal blue, azure blue, violet blue, and greenish blue. Priests, magi and shaman of many cultures have used it to enhance their spiritual powers. Lapis promotes clarity, spiritual maturity, wisdom, compassion, strength, and also balances life energies. It helps one develop a spiritually centered character and strength of will. It awakens the connection with your higher consciousness.

Snake is the spirit animal of this moon. Snake has long been maligned and misunderstood, particularly in Western cultures. In many Native American cultures, however, Snake was respected as an animal of great power. Queztecoatl, the feathered serpent of Aztecan and Mayan mythology, is a powerful symbol of transformation. Snake changes itself by shedding its skin about three times each year. When it sheds its skin, Snake seems weak and lifeless. If Snake cannot find what it needs to help pull the old skin away from itself, Snake will suffocate and die. Yet once Snake has successfully shed its skin it emerges as bigger and stronger with a renewed lease on life. Snake is also known as a messenger who will bring word from the spirit world if you will but listen. Snake can strike and kill but she can also heal. The lesson of Snake is rebirth through the rising of earth energy within.

People of Contemplation Moon possess a natural talent for self-examination. They can look deep within themselves and teach others to do so as well. They are adaptable but change may not come without pain. Once they see the benefits in shedding their old skins however, they move forward with great strength and insight. They embrace the change and do not return to old habits. Though they often seem aloof and cold-blooded they actually have a great deal of loving energy that they simply need to learn to channel properly. Contemplation Moon people need to always be conscious of maintaining balance within their lives or else their energy can run rampant in negative ways. The children of this moon often seem wise beyond their years but need a lot of guidance in learning to harness and apply the energy they possess.

Deep Snow Moon. This is a moon of deep rest and cleansing. It is the moon of middle Winter, when the Earth is silent, blanketed in a deep layer of snow. Yet this lack of outward movement does not mean a lack of activity, for this is the time when spiritual enlightenment begins to rise. Our time of contemplation and introspection has taught us to see our spiritual self and we now bring forth our spiritual consciousness.

Echinacea, also known as the purple coneflower, is the plant of Deep Snow Moon. It grows wild on the prairies of North America and is known as one of the most powerful cleansing herbs. It is a powerful blood purifier that cleanses the lymph glands and mucous membranes. The root is used medicinally either as a tonic, tea, or herb, or externally as a poultice, smudge or bath. It helps fight fevers by attacking infections. Echinacea is used extensively in alternative medicine today as an immune system booster that prevents colds and flu during the winter season.

Obsidian is the stone associated with the Deep Snow Moon. It is a grounding stone that teaches people how to respect the energy of the Earth. It is also a strong protective stone that brings clarity to one's inner emotional state. It can reflect the thoughts of another and bring these thoughts to the wearer, thus bestowing a type of clairvoyance. Some believe it can help you see into the future. As a protective stone it helps you center and ground with Mother Earth's energy and thus provides a foundation for stable future growth. There are many types of obsidian; each possesses a slightly different quality.

Goose is the spirit animal of this moon. Goose is strong and swift, traveling many thousands of miles each year in its migratory journey. When Goose returns to the northern nesting grounds in Spring, we know that Winter is coming to an end. Geese are strong traditionalists who honor the elders in the flock. They mate for life and are responsible parents, with both male and female caring for the young. They are practical in their outlook on life. While solidly grounded in the world they also possess keen vision that enables them to see beyond the horizon to distant places. The lesson of Goose is vision based in reality.

People of Deep Snow Moon can be visionary and humanitarian in nature. They search for ways to improve the lot of their fellow humans. They like to be of service to others and are capable of bringing new energy into any project. They can make transformation happen. They are also empathetic and possess a natural ability to understand others. They may have a natural gift of healing, both physical and emotional, but they often have to work to bring this ability to manifestation. Deep Snow Moon people are creative, quick to embrace new ideas and see those ideas spark into a new revolution in their field of endeavor.

Strong Winds Moon. This is the third moon of the North, when the winds blow strong and fast, signaling the change which is soon to come as all life prepares to leave the silent contemplation of Winter and burst forth with the new life of Spring.

The plant of Strong Winds Moon is the butterfly weed. A relative of the dandelion, butterfly weed is also known as milkweed. The seedpod is filled with silky seeds that resemble parachutes as they float on the wind, seeking a new place to root and grow. The root of the plant is widely known for its healing properties for lung and respiratory ailments. It promotes healing by inducing sweating and acts as a strong expectorant. It thus induces healing by forcing the body to eliminate toxins. It brings about healing through dramatic change.

Azurite is the stone of Strong Winds Moon. A basic carbonate of copper, it is often a brilliant azure blue or royal blue color. Historically, it was used by priests, magicians and shaman to increase psychic abilities and develop clairvoyance—the ability to see the future. Azurite also stimulates psychic and healing abilities, improves meditation, promotes intuition, and induces a high energy level. Azurite helps bring about a personal transformation similar to the way the chrysalis process transforms the caterpillar into a butterfly. Azurite can help you discover the way to leave the darkness of doubt and come into the light of knowledge.

Butterfly is the spirit animal of Strong Winds Moon. Butterfly is a universal symbol of hope, change and life. She represents the cycle of death, regeneration and rebirth. Butterfly begins life as a caterpillar, a multi-legged insect anchored to the earth. As a caterpillar she begins a journey to find a suitable place to build a cocoon—a chrysalis that appears to be a self-made tomb. While in its chrysalis state, Butterfly appears to be dead, yet she is undergoing a profound metamorphosis and will eventually emerge in a new form as a beautiful winged creature. Butterfly is a universal symbol of hope, change and life. Butterfly teaches us to embrace change and transformation.

The people of Strong Winds Moon often feel more comfortable with the spirit realm than with the physical plane. Like the chrysalis, they find the hidden mystic realm more comforting than the outside world. If they are well-grounded, they have the ability to be powerful shaman and travel between the two worlds. Without that grounding, however, they can become trapped in a sea of turbulent emotion and have difficulty connecting with others in this world. Strong Winds Moon people have the ability to be great healers. They often seem introverted and withdrawn but that is because they have the ability to see beyond the surface appearances of the physical world and understand the reality of spirit.

The Blue Moon

There is a phrase that goes, "That only happens once in a blue moon." Have you ever wondered what that means? A Blue Moon is the thirteenth moon of the year. It occurs when two moons fall within the same month. A Blue Moon will occur about once every two and a half years, usually in months that have thirty-one days. A Blue Moon signals a time of great change. The Blue Moon possesses tremendous power. It intensifies the qualities of the other moons of the sacred direction in which it falls.

Pyrite or fool's gold is the stone of the Blue Moon. While pyrite looks like gold, it is a different stone altogether. Unlike gold that is soft and malleable, pyrite is sharp and hard; it has no value. Thistle is the plant of Blue Moon. Every part of the thistle can be used as food or medicine. The stem and root can be peeled and eaten raw or cooked while the fruitlike seeds can be roasted. Tea made from thistle is used to cure digestive aliments, reduce fevers, expel worms, and increase activity in brain function. Yet just try to touch this plant. Its sharp teeth reach out and prick you harshly. The many offerings of thistle are thus hidden behind a most effective defense system. If you can get past these defenses, however, thistle will help you understand the different levels of reality.

Coyote, the eternal trickster, symbolizes the Blue Moon. Coyote is an animal of contradictions. A central figure of Native American myths, he at times creates the world and at other times destroys it. He is sometimes the hero and sometimes the antagonist. He is both a clown and a wise healer. Coyote thus has the ability to turn the world upside down. Coyote is a survivor who has adapted to life in many different settings, including cities such as Los Angeles and Denver. When Coyote is present, you never know what is going to happen. The lesson of Coyote is to embrace the moment and always be prepared for the unexpected.

People born under the Blue Moon are very much like Coyote. They can help you and they can heal you. Or, they can bring disorder and confusion into your life. They can be your best friend or your worst enemy. People of the Blue Moon are often volatile in temperament and prone to extremes; they can turn on you in a moment. You never know what to expect from Blue Moon people nor is it easy to truly know them. Yet, if you take the time to understand them, they can teach you the mysteries of life.

These are the thirteen moons of the Medicine Wheel. Each moon has its own lessons as exemplified by their corresponding plants, minerals and spirit animals. How well you learn the lessons these moons have to offer is up to you. In the next chapter, we will learn how to identify and communicate with the spirit animals that walk the path of the Medicine Wheel.

4

LEARNING FROM THE SPIRIT ANIMALS

In Medicine Wheel teachings, a shaman was always accompanied by spirit animals that protected and guided him. A spirit animal is a combination of the qualities of the real animal itself and the essence of the collective consciousness of that animal totem. A spirit animal thus possesses the knowledge, wisdom, strength, and power of all the animals of its species that have ever lived. Eagle thus speaks with the voice of all eagles just as Turtle is the voice of all turtles.

Spirit animals stand ready to help and teach us. They will share their knowledge and protect us with their power. As helpers and guides they come to teach us what we need to know. We must listen to them however, or they will leave. If we are willing to open ourselves to the lessons they have for us, they will walk by our side and show us the next step on the path of the Medicine Wheel.

For, as seen, each animal, each bird, each fowl,
has been so named for some peculiarity of that individual beast, bird, or fowl,
and in this manner represents some particular phase of
man's development in the earth's plane, or that consciousness
of some particular element or personality that is manifested in man.
(Edgar Cayce Reading 294-87)

Each culture has its own spirit animals that are specific to its particular habitat. There is a saying among anthropologists that, "There are no tiger gods where there are no tigers." This means that you will only find a tiger god among people who inhabit the jungle where the tiger exists; you won't find a tiger god among the Eskimo of the Aleutian Islands.

The spirit animals noted in this book are common to North America and are those that have been traditionally used in Native American Medicine Wheel teachings. There are other animals however, who possess the same qualities and teach us the same lessons. In today's world of mass communication we know of animals that live in far off lands. For example, you may have an elephant as your spirit animal, although an elephant is not native to your home state of Kansas. That doesn't mean that your connection with the elephant is any less real.

What follows is a synopsis of the animals associated with the totems and moons as discussed in previous chapters. The qualities or characteristics of each animal as well as the lessons they can teach us are given below. Following each lesson are suggested affirmations or "mantras" to help you focus on bringing that lesson into manifestation. Non-traditional "like" animals that correspond to these Native American animals are also noted, as are animals that may not be related in phylogenetic terms, but nonetheless possess similar character traits.

The Totem Animals

EAGLE *(East)*

- ➤ Qualities: clear vision; actualization of vision; guide to the spirit within; a warrior spirit; fearless; the link between Father Sky and Mother Earth; embodies the light
- ➤ Lesson: Eagle teaches us the strength and power that comes from spiritual vision.
- ➤ Like-Animals: Condor
- ➤ Affirmations to draw upon the strength and vision of Eagle:

~Fear disappears in the light of my true spirit self.
~The clarity of my higher self is evident in all aspects of my life.
~The fearless warrior within pursues the truth of life.
I AM the Light.

****

LION (COUGAR/PUMA) *(South)*

- ➤ Qualities: passion in love; power in manifestation; strength in motion
- ➤ Lesson: Lion teaches us the power of manifestation.
- ➤ Like-Animals: African Lion, Tiger, Cat (domestic), and also Jaguar. **Jaguar** is also known for the power of transformation.
- ➤ Affirmations to call upon the power of Lion:

~I live in the present and see the world as it is.
~The illusions of the world do not cloud my positive manifestations.
~I move toward the horizon and embrace the world I envision.
I AM Power in Action.

****

BEAR *(West)*

➤ Qualities: healing power of the unconsciousness; the ability to go within; responsibility; balance

➤ Lesson: Bear teaches us how to heal ourselves and others.

➤ Like-Animals: Large, predatory animals

➤ Affirmations to develop the innate healing ability of Bear:

~I bring forth my ability to heal and to create harmony and balance in life.
~The light from within illuminates the harmonious balance in my life.
~I share my healing power to help others.
~I AM the Healer.

****

BUFFALO *(North)*

➤ Qualities: wholeness; self-sacrifice; responsibility; protection; brings the gift of the Pipe

➤ Lesson: Buffalo teaches us to give of ourselves for the greater good.

➤ Like-Animals: Large, non-predatory animals such as Moose, Elk and Elephant, and also Parrot. **Parrot** possesses many of the same qualities as Buffalo.

➤ Affirmations to cultivate the selfless spirit of Buffalo:

~I give of myself for the good of those I love.
~I respect and honor my part in the wholeness of life.
~My life is a series of selfless acts.
~I AM the Peacemaker.

****

TURTLE/TORTOISE *(Center)*

> Qualities: grounded; primal connection to the Mother Earth; protection; purposeful; tenacious; survival; long life

> Lesson: Turtle teaches us intent, tenacity and patience.

> Like-Animals: Lizard

> Affirmations to call upon the resolve and patience of Turtle:

~I am grounded and connected to the Earth and honor her intentions.
~I see what needs to be done and I do it with patience and intent.
~My actions are deliberate and well measured.
~I AM Life.

The Moon Animals

HAWK *(New Buds Moon)*

> Qualities: far-sighted; deliberate foresight; connection between Father Sky and the Sungate Keeper of the Thunder Clouds; emissary to the Thunder Beings

> Lesson: Hawk teaches us foresight, deliberation and intent.

> Like-Animals: Thunderbird.

Mythic **Thunderbird** is the largest hawk. He lives with the spirits and is the messenger between the Thunder Beings and humans. He has the ability to heal people.

In Pueblo Indian mythology **Red Hawk** is esteemed to be on a par with Eagle, and able to ascend and communicate with the ancient spirits, the *katsina* (Kachinas) themselves.

> Affirmations to draw upon wisdom of Hawk:

~I utilize my gift of sight for the greater good.
~I have within me the power of healing, the power of life.
~My wings carry the prayers of earth to heaven.
~I AM the Voice of Spirit.

****

BEAVER *(Planting Moon)*

> Qualities: industrious; self-reliant; deliberate purpose; commitment; stability; balance; harmony; traditional values

> Lesson: Beaver teaches us to master the flow of the life force.

> Like-Animals: Ant

Ant is about community and strength. Ant is small but very strong and capable of carrying loads twice her size. Ant works hard for the good of the nest. Ant teaches us to work hard without complaining.

> Affirmations to learn the industriousness and balance of Beaver:

~I am in harmony with the ebb and flow of life.
~I build a full life, with commitment, one step at a time.
~I create my life within the harmony of the Universe.
~I AM Self-Reliant.

****

DEER *(New Flowers Moon)*

> Qualities: prosperity; good fortune; beauty; grace; innocence; sensitivity; heart energy

> Lesson: Deer teaches us grace, beauty and love.

> Like-Animals: Antelope, Giraffe

> Affirmations to call upon the grace of Deer:

~I walk with beauty and grace on the spiral of life.
~My heart is open to the flow of prosperity in my life.
~My prosperity flows naturally and gracefully.
~I AM Beautiful.

****

OTTER *(Hot Sun Moon)*

> Qualities: playfulness; curiosity; innocence; nurturing; devoted to home life; companionship

> Lesson: Otter teaches us to live in the moment.

➤ Like-Animals: Mouse, Raccoon

➤ Affirmations to live with the joy of Otter:

~I live life with joy and passion.
~I am compassionate in the daily activities of my life.
~I immensely enjoy my life.
~I AM Laughter.

******

STURGEON *(Hot Winds Moon)*

➤ Qualities: determination; perseverance; strength; survival; power of instinct; ancient kinship; ancient depth of knowledge; royalty; king of the fishes

➤ Lesson: Sturgeon teaches us perseverance, strength and survival.

➤ Like-Animals: Salmon, Alligator

➤ Affirmations to cultivate the inner strength of Sturgeon:

~I am guided by my inner knowledge in all I do.
~I possess the power to stand strong and endure.
~I remember the ancient ways.
~I AM Strength.

******

SPIDER *(Harvest Moon)*

➤ Qualities: resourcefulness; creativity; patience; trust; faith; beauty; harmony

➤ Lesson: Spider teaches us that all life is connected.

➤ Like-Animals: Honey Bee, Bumble Bee

➤ Affirmations to understand the creative and unifying perspective of Spider:

~ I create the life I live.
~I patiently weave beauty into my life.
~The creative power of life lies deep within me.
~I AM Harmony.

******

WOLF *(Hunters Moon)*

➤ Qualities: self-will; loyalty to the family group; master of relationships; selflessness; trust; honesty

➤ Lesson: Wolf teaches us the strength and power of the collective consciousness.

➤ Like-Animals: Dog

Dog is the domesticated Wolf. Dog manifests loyalty and protection. He sees us as we are yet loves us anyway. Dog faces death with bravery and shows us how to be brave in the face of adversity. Dog teaches us unconditional love.

➤ Affirmations to foster the loyalty and unconditional love of Wolf within self:

~I will sacrifice self for the higher good.
~Selfless actions characterize my relationships.
~My power comes from selfless devotion to those I love.
~I AM Loyal and Faithful.

****

OWL *(First Freeze Moon)*

➤ Qualities: inner vision; self-examination; mystery; knowledge of the spirit world; embodies the shadow/darkness; strong medicine; transmitter of the Old Knowledge and Wisdom (the female aspect); a messenger; an omen

➤ Lesson: Owl teaches us the truth of inner vision.

➤ Like-Animals: Raven, Crow

In Pueblo tradition, **Raven** is a messenger from the *katsinas* (Kachinas).

➤ Affirmations to bring forth our inner wisdom of the ancient truths:

~I look within myself to face my fear and overcome it.
~I respect the mysteries of life.
~I embrace the darkness and learn from its hidden wisdom.
~I AM Wisdom.

****

HORSE *(Silent Snow Moon)*

➤ Qualities: travel; partnership; vehicle to the spirit world; control of power

➤ Lesson: Horse teaches us how to travel to the spirit world.

➤ Like-Animals: Dolphin, Whale

Dolphin and **Whale** represent intelligence, communication, purity, and giving. They are guardians to the spirits who journey to other worlds. They teach us that we are measured not by what we have, but by what we give.

➤ Affirmations to help us see beyond the veil of the physical world and glimpse the world of spirit:

~My personal embodiment of spirit guides me on the path of life.
~I see through the veils of this world and travel fearlessly to the spirit realm.
~My strides are steady as I move forward on the path of enlightenment.
~I AM a companion to others on the spiritual journey.

****

SNAKE *(Contemplation Moon)*

➤ Qualities: transformation; renewal; mystery; life energy; rising passion within

➤ Lesson: Snake teaches us the lesson of rebirth through the rising of earth energy within.

➤ Like Animals: none

➤ Affirmations to raise the kundalini force within:

~I release old habits, attitudes and beliefs and I am reborn anew.
~As I shed my physical illusions, I awaken to a new and higher level of awareness.
~I possess the willingness to change as I grow in spiritual knowledge.
~I AM Creative.

****

GOOSE *(Deep Snow Moon)*

➤ Qualities: sustenance; gregarious; stability; community; tradition

➤ Lesson: Goose teaches us the power of family and community bonds.

➢ Like-Animals: Rabbit

➢ Affirmations to help understand the value of community:

> *~I grow strong through my relationship with family and friends.*
> *~I provide for those who depend upon me.*
> *~I respect my origins and continually learn from my past experiences.*
> *~ I AM Centered and Focused.*

****

BUTTERFLY *(Strong Winds Moon)*

➢ Qualities: regeneration; transformation; hope; fearlessness

➢ Lesson: Butterfly teaches us to embrace change and transformation.

➢ Like-Animals: Egyptian Scarab

➢ Affirmations to foster a spirit of transformation:

> *~As the winds bring change I accept my fate.*
> *~ Life is eternal. Through change, I am continually being reborn.*
> *~Death is only a stepping stone on the path of transformation.*
> *~I AM Eternal.*

****

COYOTE *(Blue Moon)*

➢ Qualities: wily humor; new thought; trust; adaptable; growth through change; disorder; a paradox; knowledge of the light and the darkness; the trickster

➢ Lesson: Coyote teaches us to live in the now and be prepared for the unexpected.

➢ Like Animals: Fox

➢ Affirmations to live in the present moment:

> *~I live in the now.*
> *~I accept life as it is with a smile on my face.*
> *~I never take life too seriously.*
> *~I AM a Free Spirit.*

Recognizing Your Spirit Animal

Each person has a natal spirit animal that is always with you and is related to your soul's purpose in the earth plane. Another constant companion is a "clan" animal that has a special connection with you and your ancestors. You will also have one or more animals that come and go throughout your life as you face and resolve certain issues.

Our spirit animals often visit us in dreams and in meditation. In fact, as you walk the path of the Medicine Wheel and meet your spirit animals, you will likely realize that they have already appeared to you in some way. By walking the path however, you develop a close connection with these guides and teachers, and learn to communicate with them.

When you first embark upon the Medicine Wheel path, you will find that you encounter "signs" along the way—instances of synchronicity that alert you to the animals that surround you. You may run across a particular stuffed animal, see a tee-shirt with an animal print, or simply think of an animal that has not previously been a part of your life. If you run across several signs or encounter one sign repeatedly, you can be sure that animal is trying to speak with you.

These signs are messages from your spirit animals; they are trying to get your attention and make you realize that they are there if you but stop and look beyond the noise and clutter of the physical world. For these animals are found not only in spirit or seen only in dreams or visions. Spirit animals can appear to us in the physical world as well. All things in spirit are reflected in the physical world.

You may find yourself drawn to an animal that has a quality that you admire but do not possess. Such an animal usually has a lesson for you. Or, you may meet an animal that has a quality that is a reflection of yourself. That animal is connected to you in some way and is waiting to speak with you.

When spirit animals speak, they can speak with or without words. They may communicate through feelings or emotion, give you a dream, or show you a vision. By listening to what these animals have to say and observing the way they live and interact with the world around them, we can learn more about ourselves, our relationships to others, and our place in the world itself.

If you talk to the animals they will talk with you and you will know each other.
If you do not talk to them you will not know them,
and what you do not know you will fear. What one fears one destroys.
~Chief Dan George

5

BUILDING YOUR PERSONAL
MEDICINE WHEEL

B uilding a Medicine Wheel is a very personal activity that will be tempered by your desires
and purpose. There is no one way of building a wheel that is more right or wrong
than another. The information given here is intended to be used as guidelines. Follow the
suggestions given below as just that—suggestions. When building your wheel, do what you
feel is right. Use your intuition to help you build your Medicine Wheel.

A Medicine Wheel can be permanent (long-term), temporary (short-term), or momentary
(immediately disassembled after one use). You do not need a large outdoor space to construct
your wheel. A small wheel can be built on a dresser top or coffee table in an apartment. You
can build an elaborate wheel with thirty-plus stones or a simple wheel with five stones. You
can construct your wheel by yourself or enlist the aid of others. Whatever type of Medicine
Wheel you construct however, consider your actions to be a ceremonial act.

Location and Size

Choose a location that feels right, powerful, and safe. If building your wheel outside,
choose an area that is private and not prone to disturbance by visitors. Outside areas need
to be fairly flat as well. If you are building an indoor wheel, choose a location in your house
or apartment that has the right feeling and is fairly isolated from constant daily activity or
frequent disruption. You may want to meditate to obtain guidance in choosing the right
location for your wheel.

Determine the size of your wheel. Do you want to be able to literally walk around the wheel? If so, you need to make sure it is large enough to accommodate you stepping through the quadrants. You don't need an outside area to make a large wheel. A spare bedroom or dining room with the table moved to the side can accommodate a six to eight foot wheel that is large enough to walk through.

Choosing the Stones

The minimum number of stones needed to construct a Medicine Wheel is five, one for each of the sacred four directions and one for the center stone. A more traditional wheel requires seventeen stones, the five mentioned above plus an additional twelve stones, one for each of the moons. A twenty-one stone wheel adds one stone each for Mother Earth, Grandfather Sun, Father Sky, and Grandmother Moon. A very complex Medicine Wheel adds an additional twelve stones for the spirit paths and four stones for the elemental totem clans. For our purposes, we will focus on a traditional wheel of seventeen stones.

The type of stones you choose will depend upon the kind of wheel you plan to build. A large outdoor wheel would be best if built with large rocks that are easily seen when you walk the wheel. If you are choosing your rocks from the surrounding area, choose rocks that call to you or that "feel" right. Ask permission before you take the rock. If you get a funny feeling, leave that rock and choose another. *Always* leave an offering of tobacco, corn meal, sage, or something similar for each rock you take. This is simply proper respect for the spirits of the area. Prior to the ceremony, gather your rocks together and place them next to the spot you plan to construct your wheel.

An indoor wheel can be constructed with rocks or smaller stones taken from the outdoors as described above. You can also use marbles or purchase different colored stones from a craft store or even an aquarium shop. If you don't have the means to either choose rocks from outdoors or buy the stones, you can cut out a circular or oval shape from different colored papers and use those cutouts as the stones for an indoor wheel. Feel free to write the names of the directions and the moons on the paper pieces as reference when you construct the wheel.

Some people may have the time and means to collect the specific types of stones that are associated with each direction and moon. This can be expensive, however. If you feel so moved, by all means do so. But know that this is not necessary. The power of the Medicine Wheel does not depend upon the type of rock, stone, pebble, or paper you use in its construction. The power of the sacred circle is much greater than that. It is inherent in the traditions and teachings of the Medicine Wheel as practiced by generations of people across time and space.

The Ceremony

Grounding and Centering. Prior to constructing the wheel, bless and sanctify the ground/area upon which you will build your wheel. Stand in the center of the wheel, or next to the location if building a small wheel on a tabletop. Ground and center yourself by taking a few deep breaths and calming your mind. Feel your connection to Mother Earth. Imagine roots growing from your spine down through your legs and connecting with the Earth herself. Offer a prayer of thanksgiving for the opportunity to commune with the spirit world.

Protection and Cleansing. Using a sage stick or incense, smudge yourself by invoking the spirits of protection and cleansing. Also smudge any participants, the rocks and the area where you intend to build the wheel. If you do not have a sage stick or incense, you can use a feather in the same way. Or, you can simply wave your arms and invoke the spirits of protection and cleansing. I recommend using a clockwise motion while cleansing the area and asking for protection.

Prayerful Intent. Following the smudging, take a moment of silence to again center yourself. Offer a prayer to the Creative Spirit and ask for guidance in constructing your Medicine Wheel. Express your intent and what you hope to accomplish by building this wheel.

Placement and Blessings.

The Center Stone. Pick up the stone of the Center, bless it, thank it, and offer it to the Creative Spirit. Place it in its designated spot in the Center of your wheel. Say a prayer of thanksgiving for the guidance the stone will bring. Place an offering of corn meal, tobacco, sage, or other appropriate offering near the stone. Offer this to the sprits and to the place. Note: You may offer corn meal or tobacco after you place each stone, or you may make one offering when you lay the final stone.

Stones for the Sacred Four Directions. Using your knowledge of the directions, or a compass if you have one, begin to lay your wheel in each of the four directions. Begin in the East and follow the wheel in a clockwise direction, laying stones for the South, West, and North respectively. Each stone should be blessed, thanked and offered to the Creative Spirit in turn.

The Moon Stones. Begin again in the East. Lay one stone for each of the East moons. Then move to the South and lay the stones for the South moons, then the West moons and finally the North moons. Again, each stone should be blessed, thanked and offered to the Creative Spirit.

Final Blessing. When you have finished placing the stones, return to the Center and offer a final prayer, honoring the sacred four directions, the twelve moons, and the Creative Spirit. Ask the spirits to bless your Medicine Wheel. Then leave the wheel. The ceremony is concluded.

A description of this ceremony along with a Medicine Wheel diagram is included in the Appendix of the workbook. It provides a handy, one-page reference guide you can use when building your Medicine Wheel.

Adaptations

The Medicine Wheel Ceremony described above can be adapted to any circumstance and situation, including the size of the area and the number of people involved in its construction. Medicine wheels can be built with flower petals, seashells, pinecones, acorns, or any other material that is readily available. You can vary the number of stones depending upon the time you can devote to construction. If you are traveling, you may want to build a five stone wheel with small stones that you can easily pack into a small pouch. After you are comfortable in building the seventeen stone wheel described above, you may want to expand by adding stones for Mother Earth, Father Sky, Grandfather Sun, and Grandmother Moon. If you are interested in building more elaborate wheels, I refer you to the writings of Sun Bear.

Once your wheel is finished, it will change the energy of the area in which it is built and influence the creatures that reside nearby. Any Medicine Wheel will immediately begin to send healing energy to the Earth around it. The more you use your wheel, the more energy it will build up and pass on to the Earth and her creatures. If you have built an indoor wheel, it will steadily raise the vibration of your home. By building a Medicine Wheel, you become part of a centuries old power tradition. You tap into an inexhaustible source of nature energy that has been helping to heal and guide people for thousands of years.

6

THE MEDICINE WHEEL AS A TOOL
FOR SPIRITUAL GROWTH

Many of the world's great religions, including Hinduism, Buddhism, Judaism, Zoroastrianism, Christianity, and Islam, teach that there is only one God, one Creative Spirit, one Spiritual Source, or one power higher than ourselves. This God has been known by many names and has been worshipped in many ways throughout human history.

The Great Teachers have shown us that the highest level of spiritual attainment is the realization that we are one with this Creative Spirit. They have also left us knowledge of different tools and techniques by which we can attune the body, mind and soul so we may attain a level of consciousness at which we understand our unity with God. The path of the Medicine Wheel is but one means of achieving spiritual attunement. It is one tool among many that we may use to help us on our long journey home.

Walking the Path

If you are reading this book you are already drawn to the path of the Medicine Wheel. You need only make the decision as to whether this is a path you choose to follow. Once you decide to walk this path, you can begin your journey by following these basic steps.

> ➢ *Learn the major teachings of the wheel and integrate them into your life.*
> ➢ *Study the teachings of the sacred four directions and the Center. Understand the meaning of the elements, the seasons and the cycles of the day.*
> ➢ *Know the plant and stone of each direction. Honor the totem animals.*

The teachings of the Medicine Wheel are based on a nature-centered form of spirituality that acknowledges our kinship with all living creatures upon the Earth as well as our connection with the plant and mineral kingdoms. It also recognizes our relationship with nature's elements and the celestial bodies in the heavens. When you align yourself with the teachings of the Medicine Wheel you are grounded in a holistic foundation that sees all life as one. This is the teaching of UNITY.

> ➤ *Identify your natal position on the wheel and the moon under which you were born.*
>
> ➤ *Come to know your natal spirit animal, plant and stone. Embrace the lessons they have for you.*

By learning about your natal position on the wheel, the moon under which you were born and the spirit animal that guides your path, you discover insights into your deepest self. Through introspection, you learn about your attitudes and emotions, the "whys" of relationships, and long-buried inner beliefs and thoughts. You will even come to understand the reasons for your physical strengths and weaknesses.

> ➤ *Discover your current position on the wheel. Know the moon that most influences you now. Know the lessons associated with this place on the wheel.*
>
> ➤ *Meet the spirit animals that are currently working with you. Seek out the lessons they can teach.*

By attuning yourself to your present position on the wheel, you can take the knowledge gained from your natal position and apply it to the current circumstances, situations and relationships you are experiencing today. You begin the process of introspection—self-analysis. It takes courage to look within and examine self. But as you do so, you begin to truly integrate the physical, mental, emotional, and spiritual aspects of your being. You learn how to heal yourself and so begin to heal your relationships with others. You take the first steps toward becoming a fully integrated, spiritually centered being. This is the teaching of BALANCE and HARMONY.

> ➤ *Build a Medicine Wheel. Learn to travel the wheel.*

Medicine Wheel teachings make it clear that to remain where you were born on the wheel or to reside in a place that is comfortable but not challenging means you stagnate and fail to move forward to higher levels of spiritual attunement. For those who choose to do this, their journey on Earth becomes little more than an existence rather than a life well lived with joy, passion and love. Through the teachings of the Medicine Wheel you learn to take charge and begin to chart the course for your life rather than being buffeted by the winds of fortune. You understand that nothing stays the same—all life changes into something more. This is the teaching of MOVEMENT and GROWTH.

> ➤ *Apply the lessons you have learned while traveling the path of the Medicine Wheel.*

In your travels around the Medicine Wheel, you come to understand the wonderful gifts that each lesson has to offer. You realize that opposites are really different notes of the same harmony. You know that the knowledge and wisdom you gain, even during difficult times, will lead you to a closer relationship with the Creative Spirit. You learn to live in the moment and work with the ever-changing spirals of the web of life rather than fighting against them. You trust that the Creative Spirit is taking care of you and will provide for all your needs. You begin to rely less on human sight and see instead with spiritual vision. Eventually you recognize that you are spirit! This is the teaching of ATTUNEMENT.

Unity, balance, harmony, movement, growth, and attunement—these are the major teachings of the Medicine Wheel; all other lessons stem from these. The exercises in the following section are designed to help you with these steps and acquaint you with the power and energy of the Medicine Wheel. Use them as you move forward on your journey.

Guidance in Daily Life

The Creative Spirit always speaks to us, every moment of every day. Many people are aware that God speaks to us in our dreams, during meditation and while we are in prayer. But God also speaks to us in those busy moments of ordinary life. Spirit speaks to us through symbolic images and patterns and also through synchronicity—those so-called "coincidences" that consistently recur in our lives. We become so caught up in the drama of the moment, however, that we fail to recognize the guidance we are given.

By walking the path of the Medicine Wheel you become more attuned to spirit, and hence more aware of the signs and symbols you encounter on life's path. You come to understand the significance of synchronistic events in your life. You learn to recognize spiritual guidance when it is given to you. More importantly, you learn to act on the guidance you are given.

Making the decision to follow a spiritual path—any spiritual path—will forever change your life. The path of the Medicine Wheel is no exception. Once you know its teachings and feel its power you cannot return to who you were before. Even if you abandon the path for a time, it will continue to call to you.

The Medicine Wheel is more than just a sacred circle. It is an ever-ascending spiral that continually moves upward toward God. Once you complete one revolution you move on to the next spiral and continue forward. Spiritual enlightenment is a journey that leads us around and around, yet ever upward to the light of the Creative Spirit. I wish you well on your journey home.

> *The first peace, which is the most important,*
> *is that which comes from within the souls of men*
> *when they realize their relationship, their oneness, with the universe and all its*
> *powers, and when they realize that at the center of the universe dwells Wakan-Tanka*
> *and that this center is really everywhere, it is within each of us.*
> *This is the real peace, and the others are but reflections of this.*
> *The second peace is that which is made between two individuals,*
> *and the third is that which is made between two nations.*
> *But above all you should understand that there can never be peace between nations*
> *until there is first known that true peace which is within the souls of men.*
> *~Black Elk*

EXERCISES

The exercises that follow are designed to help you create sacred space. They are tools to help you *experience* the power and energy of the Medicine Wheel. They are "ceremony" and should be considered as such.

You will note that the opening steps for each exercise are similar. It is very important that each visualization, guided imagery, meditation, or physical movement upon the Medicine Wheel begins with grounding and protection. Use your own prayer of protection if you prefer.

These exercises will introduce you to the teachings of the Medicine Wheel, help you meet your teachers and guides and most importantly help you discover more about yourself. The exercises given here are just guidelines. Feel free to adapt them as you see fit. You can modify them or create your own ceremony. A Medicine Wheel can be built for any specific intent such as finding your life's purpose, physical healing, manifesting a vision, to bring harmony to relationships, to increase your energy, to invoke protection, or to help you manifest something specific in your life. As you spend time upon the Medicine Wheel path, you will personalize and expand upon the exercises presented here.

Prior to beginning the ceremony, you may wish to smudge yourself and the Medicine Wheel. You may also use music, shake a rattle, beat a drum, or burn incense as a means of preparing your sacred space. Do what feels right to *you*.

The time you spend on each exercise is also up to you. Some people may spend no more than ten minutes while others will exceed an hour. That does not mean the hour journey was "better" than the ten minute one; each individual is just that—a unique individual—and the time you spend on the wheel will vary. You determine how fast you move and when the exercise is concluded.

I suggest that you take some time following each exercise to reflect upon your experience, focusing particularly upon the teachings you have been shown and how you can apply those lessons in your life. What have you learned about yourself that you didn't know before? What have you learned about your relationships with others? Was there a lesson in the teachings that confirmed something you suspected but did not know for sure? How can you use the information you gathered to create positive change in your life? Each exercise is followed by a "reflections" note page designed to help you codify and record your thoughts.

I also highly encourage you to record the experiences of your journey along the Medicine Wheel path. If you do not currently keep a journal, I suggest you start one. Try to record your experiences immediately afterward, when the information is fresh in your mind. Medicine Wheel journeys are sometimes like dreams and have a tendency to slip from memory as time passes. Remember, you must master the lessons you are given before you can be shown the next step forward on your journey.

Exercise One: Attunement to the Teachings of the Medicine Wheel

This visualization will help you attune to the wisdom and knowledge that lie within the sacred circle. It will introduce you to the teachers and guides that await you upon this path. It will teach you to open your heart to the sacred teachings of the Medicine Wheel.

Visualize yourself at the Center of your Medicine Wheel. Close your eyes and take a moment of silence to center yourself and quiet your mind. Release the cares and worries you carry with you. Slow your breathing and be still. Surround yourself with the White Light of Protection. Acknowledge the presence of the Great Spirit and offer thanks for his presence.

Feel your connection to Mother Earth. Imagine roots extending from your feet and growing slowly down into the ground. Be anchored in your connection to the Center. Feel the strength and unity that flows from Mother Earth to all her children.

Invite the powers of the sacred four directions to speak to you. Feel the fresh winds of the East as they show you the way of a new beginning. Feel the strong winds of the South as they bring you the power of understanding. Feel the healing winds of the West as they swirl around you. Feel the gentle winds of the North as they teach you to look within.

Invite the powers of the elements to share their knowledge with you. Feel the breath of Air, the warmth of Fire, the coolness of Water, and the strength of Earth. See the seasons pass in their eternal cycle: Spring to Summer to Autumn to Winter, and again to Spring. Follow the journey of Grandfather Sun and Grandmother Moon as they travel across the heavens from Sunrise to Noon to Sunset to Midnight. Feel the ebb and flow of energy as it circles through the rhythms of life. Understand that life is movement, change and growth.

Open your heart to the sacred teachings of the Medicine Wheel. Understand the harmony and balance that come from being in attunement with all things that live upon Mother Earth. Hear her voice. Honor the trees, the plants and the stones. They are your brothers and sisters. Honor the animals. They are your teachers.

Honor the ancient ones who have gone before. They are your mothers and fathers who have given you life. Invite them to speak. Ask them to share their wisdom. Call upon the spirits to come to you. Ask them to bless you. Quiet your soul so you may hear them and receive their gifts. Thank them for coming to you.

Hear the song of creation, the melody that brought all things into being. Feel your kinship with all that is. Feel peace and joy and love flowing through you. Feel safe and protected in the sacred circle of the Medicine Wheel. Spend some time in the quiet solitude of this peace, wrapped safely in the mantle of Mother Earth's love. When you are ready, slowly return to a state of waking consciousness.

Know that you have been in a sacred space. The Great Sprit has touched you and you are forever changed. You are born anew in the sacred circle. You see within your own soul and you know who you are.

Your heart is now open to the sacred teachings of the Medicine Wheel.

Reflections on the Teachings of the Medicine Wheel

When I grounded myself and connected to Mother Earth, I felt:

When the winds of the sacred four directions blew over me, I:

As the rhythms of life flowed through me, I:

As I opened my heart to the wisdom of the sacred teachings, I (explore your feelings):

The ancient ones and spirits shared this message with me:

Standing in unity with all creation, I (explain how you felt, what you thought):

My time in this sacred space has changed and transformed me. I now (record how you have changed):

Date: _____

Exercise Two: Identifying Your Present Place on the Medicine Wheel

This exercise will help you identify your current position on the wheel. It will bring to you the teachers and lessons you need most at this time in your life. It can be done as a physical activity with a large medicine wheel or as a mental visualization. If you use it as visualization, imagine a Medicine Wheel in your mind's eye. The steps are the same in the physical or mental activity.

If you are walking the wheel, place an offering at the Center. Then return to a point outside the circle. Close your eyes and take a moment of silence to center yourself. Slow your breathing and still your mind. Surround yourself with the White Light of Protection. Ground yourself. Imagine roots growing from your feet and reaching down into the ground. Feel your connection to Mother Earth. Acknowledge the presence of the Great Spirit and offer thanks for his presence.

Enter the circle from the East, as you are seeking a new beginning. Circle the wheel clockwise at least one time. Begin a second circle, this time moving more slowly. As you circle, ask the position that is most affecting your life to reach out and speak to you.

Observe your reactions as you move about the wheel. You may feel a pull toward a particular place or you may feel a hand pushing you into a certain position. You may be hot or cold, or perhaps you will feel a chill run up and down your spine as you draw near to a particular stone. You may feel light-headed or a surge of strength at one point. Be aware of sounds and smells. If a spirit animal appears, go where he leads you.

Keep circling the Medicine Wheel in this manner until it is clear which stone is calling to you. Sit next to this stone.   Note the sacred direction to which this stone belongs. Ask the stone how it is influencing your life. Is it influencing you on the physical, mental, emotional, or spiritual level? Perhaps it is impacting you on more than one level or even all four. Reflect on the element, season, and day cycle this stone represents. Acknowledge its moon and ask it to share the lessons it holds for you.

Speak to the other teachers of this position. Speak to the totem clan, the plant and the spirit animal. Ask them to share the lessons they have for you. Ask their help in learning these lessons and applying them in your life. Wait for their answer. Stay as long as necessary. When you believe you have received all they have to offer at this time, say a prayer of thanksgiving and leave an offering. Complete your circle and exit in the East.

If you feel there is more information for you, you may want to repeat these steps until you have found your current position on the wheel for the physical, mental, emotional, and spiritual levels of your being. You may do this immediately afterward or repeat the process on another day. Do what feels right to you. Do continue the process until you have identified your position for all four levels.

Conclude each walk with an offering to the stone and the teachers that speak to you, the places on the wheel that are working with you, and the wheel itself. Thank the Great Spirit.

Record your experiences.

Reflections on My Place on the Medicine Wheel

As I walked the Medicine Wheel, the direction to which I was drawn was:

This direction represents:

I felt the following sensory perceptions as I walked the wheel:

I saw or felt the presence of a spirit animal(s):

The stone of the _____ Moon called to me.

The meaning of this Moon is:

Other teachers that came to me were:

The lesson(s) this place on the Medicine Wheel holds for me is/are:

After this experience, I feel and know:

I now have knowledge that will help me to:

Date: _____

Exercise Three: Meeting Your Spirit Animals

This exercise is designed to help you meet the spirit animals that are currently walking with you. Remember that your natal spirit animal is always with you. In fact, that animal may appear to you during this exercise and introduce you to other spirit animals that are guiding you at this time. As with Exercise Two, this can be done as a visualization or by actually walking the wheel.

Keep in mind that spirit animals rarely jump out and say, "Hi, here I am." Although this may happen, they more often hide in the shadows waiting to see if you are ready to recognize them. They will test you to see if you are ready for the lessons they have to share.

Begin in the Center. Slow your breathing and quiet your mind. Close your eyes and center yourself. Place the White Light of Protection around yourself. Ground and center yourself with Mother Earth. Feel your connection to all living creatures. Acknowledge the presence of the Great Spirit and thank him for all he has given to you.

If you are walking the wheel, place an offering at the Center. Move out from the Center to the North or to the East. Walk the wheel clockwise at least one time. Begin a second circle and move to your natal position on the wheel. When you reach the stone of your birth position, stop and open yourself to the landscape that is Mother Earth. Picture the full beauty of nature, be it a forest, jungle, desert, mountaintop, or even your backyard.

Ask your natal spirit animal to come to you. Offer thanks when he/she appears. Explain your purpose for entering the sacred circle. Ask what lessons he/she has for you at this time. Listen. Ask if there are other spirit animals working with you now. If the answer is yes, ask your natal spirit animal to help you find the others.

Pay attention to your surroundings. Begin with the sky. What do you see there? Is there a bird in flight or perhaps perched in the tallest tree? Bring your sight downward to the trees. Is there an animal in the branches? Look about you. Might there be an animal deep in the bushes or hiding in the grass? Study the rocks on the ground. Our smallest teachers are tiny and sometimes very hard to see. Is there a stream or river nearby? Might your spirit animal be there? Focus on the horizon as well as the ground near your feet. Survey the entire landscape. Look with spiritual vision rather than human sight. If you do not see an animal, repeat the process.

As you do this, one or more spirit animals may appear. Ask them what lessons they have for you. Listen to what they have to say. When they have finished speaking, thank them. Also thank your natal spirit animal.

Say a prayer of thanksgiving or leave an offering. Complete your circle and exit at the direction in which you entered. Thank the Great Spirit.

Record your experiences.

Reflections on My Spirit Animals

My Natal Moon is:

The spirit animal of my Natal Moon is:

My natal spirit animal spoke to me and said:

As I looked at my surroundings, I saw (list the spirit animals):

The spirit animals that came to me shared the following lessons/information:

The information I received will help me resolve these issues in my life:

The spirit animal which is guiding me most at this time is:

The lessons I learn from _____ will help me to:
                            (spirit animal)

Date: _____

Exercise Four: Using the Medicine Wheel for Guidance

This exercise will aid you in making decisions with respect to current issues in your life. It will bring guidance and clarity to the issue and show you the path of right action. It can be completed as visualization or by actually walking the Medicine Wheel.

Begin in the Center. If you are walking the wheel, place an offering at the Center stone. Relax, close your eyes and center and ground yourself. Slow your breathing and still your mind. Surround yourself with protection. Acknowledge the presence of the Great Spirit and give him thanks.

Move to a point outside the circle and enter from the North. Circle the wheel clockwise at least once, returning to the North. Face the Center and offer your issue to the Medicine Wheel. Ask your spirit animals to come to you. Ask the ancient ones to meet you in the wheel. Ask them for guidance. Listen to what they say.

Spend some time in reflection. Consider the issue at hand. What are your choices? What have the spirit animals told you? What have the ancient ones said? Look to the East to see the path of a new beginning. Look to the South for understanding on how to manifest the highest good in this situation. Look to the West to see the outcome of your choices. Return to the North and think on these things.

Move to the Center. Feel the energy of the wheel spiral around you. Feel the power of the teachings move through you. Imagine yourself being filled with the wisdom and knowledge of all the teachers that are and all that have been. See yourself shining with the light of balance, harmony and understanding. You are in attunement with all of Earth's creations. You are at peace. And in this peace lies your answer.

Hold the answer in your heart. Look to the East for the new beginning that will come from this action. Look to the South to see what results will manifest in your life if you follow that path. Look to the West to see the ending. Look to the North and consider all that you have been shown. Look deep within your soul and know the right action you must take.

Say a prayer of thanksgiving to those that have helped you. Acknowledge your spirit animals and the ancient ones. Acknowledge the sacred four directions and the teachings they have shared. Leave an offering to all.

Move from the Center to the North and walk around the wheel once again, exiting in the East. Ask the winds of the East to help you begin this action. The East represents your commitment to carry out this action in the ordinary world. Thank the Great Spirit for the guidance he has given. Ask for the strength and courage to walk the road of right action. Thank the Medicine Wheel for her teachings.

Record your experiences.

Using the Medicine Wheel for Guidance

Issue:

As I walked the Medicine Wheel, I saw (list the spirit animals):

This was their message:

The ancient ones appeared to me. This was their message:

As I attuned my heart to the voices of my teachers, I saw the choices that lay before me:

The consequences of each choice are:

The choice that represents the highest good for me and all others is:

Following my visit to the Medicine Wheel, I resolve to:

Date: _____

Using the Medicine Wheel for Guidance

Issue:

As I walked the Medicine Wheel, I saw (list the spirit animals):

This was their message:

The ancient ones appeared to me. This was their message:

As I attuned my heart to the voices of my teachers, I saw the choices that lay before me:

The consequences of each choice are:

The choice that represents the highest good for me and all others is:

Following my visit to the Medicine Wheel, I resolve to:

Date: _____

Using the Medicine Wheel for Guidance

Issue:

As I walked the Medicine Wheel, I saw (list the spirit animals):

This was their message:

The ancient ones appeared to me. This was their message:

As I attuned my heart to the voices of my teachers, I saw the choices that lay before me:

The consequences of each choice are:

The choice that represents the highest good for me and all others is:

Following my visit to the Medicine Wheel, I resolve to:

Date: _____

APPENDIX

DIRECTION	ELEMENT	COLOR	SEASON	CYCLE	PLANT	STONE	TOTEM	MOON	ANIMAL
EAST New Beginnings Change *PHYSICAL*	AIR	YELLOW	SPRING	SUNRISE	KINNICK-KINNICK	AMBER	EAGLE	NEW BUDS (21MAR-19APR) PLANTING (20APR-20MAY) NEW FLOWERS (21MAY-20JUN)	HAWK BEAVER DEER
SOUTH Manifestation Understanding *MENTAL*	FIRE	RED	SUMMER	NOON	SWEET GRASS	GARNET	LION	HOT SUN (21JUN-22JUL) HOT WINDS (23JUL-22AUG) HARVEST (23AUG-22SEP)	OTTER STURGEON SPIDER
WEST Completion Healing *EMOTIONS*	WATER	BLUE SAPPHIRE	AUTUMN	SUNSET	SAGE	TURQUOISE	BEAR	HUNTERS (23SEP-23OCT) FIRST FREEZE (24OCT-21NOV) SILENT SNOW (22NOV-21DEC)	WOLF OWL HORSE
NORTH Grounding Contemplation *SPIRIT*	EARTH	WHITE	WINTER	MIDNIGHT	CEDAR	CLEAR QUARTZ	BUFFALO	CONTEMPLATION (22DEC-19JAN) DEEP SNOW (20JAN-18FEB) STRONG WINDS (19FEB-20MAR)	SNAKE GOOSE BUTTERFLY

THE CENTER: Represents the Creator, the origin of all things. Its correspondences are **TURTLE, OAK TREE** and **PETRIFIED WOOD**.

Table 1. Medicine Wheel Correspondences

DIRECTION	MOON	ANIMAL	PLANT	STONE
EAST	NEW BUDS (21MAR-19APR) PLANTING (20APR-20MAY) NEW FLOWERS (21MAY-20JUN)	HAWK BEAVER DEER	RED CLOVER DANDELION APPLE BLOSSOM	FIRE OPAL CITRINE CORAL
SOUTH	HOT SUN (21JUN-22JUL) HOT WINDS (23JUL-22AUG) HARVEST (23AUG-22SEP)	OTTER STURGEON SPIDER	WILD ROSE RASPBERRY SUN FLOWER	ROSE QUARTZ CARNELIAN FLUORITE
WEST	HUNTERS (23SEP-23OCT) FIRST FREEZE (24OCT-21NOV) SILENT SNOW (22NOV-21DEC)	WOLF OWL HORSE	BEARBERRY MULLEIN BIRCH TREE	JASPER MALACHITE HEMATITE
NORTH	CONTEMPLATION (22DEC-19JAN) DEEP SNOW (20JAN-18FEB) STRONG WINDS (19FEB-20MAR)	SNAKE GOOSE BUTTERFLY	CHAMOMILE ECHINACEA BUTTERFLY WEED	LAPIS LAZULI OBSIDIAN AZURITE
	BLUE MOON	COYOTE	THISTLE	PYRITE (FOOL'S GOLD)

Table 2. Moons of the Medicine Wheel

Reference Guide: Constructing a Medicine Wheel

Step One: Grounding and Centering. Bless and sanctify the ground/area upon which you will build your wheel. Stand in the center of the wheel, or next to the location if building a small wheel on a tabletop. Ground and center yourself by taking a few deep breaths and calming your mind. Feel your connection to Mother Earth; imagine roots growing from your spine, down your legs and connecting with the Earth herself. Offer a prayer of thanksgiving for the opportunity to commune with the spirit world.

Step Two: Protection and Cleansing. Using a sage stick, incense or a feather, smudge (clockwise motion) by invoking the spirits of protection and cleansing. Also smudge any participants, the rocks, and the area where you intend to build the wheel. Invoke the spirits of protection and cleansing.

Step Three: Prayer. Take a moment of silence to center yourself. Offer a prayer to the Creative Spirit and ask for guidance in constructing your Medicine Wheel. Express your intent and what you hope to accomplish by building this wheel.

Step Four: Place the Center Stone. Pick up the stone of the Center, bless it, thank it, and offer it to the Creative Spirit. Place it in its designated spot in the Center of your wheel. Say a prayer of thanksgiving for the guidance the stone will bring. Place an offering of corn meal, tobacco, sage, or other appropriate offering near the stone. Offer this to the spirits and to the place. Note: You may offer corn meal or tobacco after you place each stone, or you may make one offering when you lay the final stone.

Step Five: Place the Stones for the Sacred Four Directions. Using your knowledge of the directions, or a compass if you have one, begin to lay your wheel in each of the sacred four directions. Begin in the East and follow the wheel in a clockwise direction, laying stones for the South, West, and North respectively. Bless and thank each stone and offer it to the Creative Spirit in turn.

Step Six: Place the Moon Stones. Begin again in the East. Lay one stone for each of the East moons. Then move to the South and lay the stones for the South moons, then the West moons and finally the North moons. Again, bless and thank each stone and then offer it to the Creative Spirit.

Step Seven: Final Blessing. Return to the center and offer a final prayer, honoring the sacred four directions, the twelve moons, and the Creative Spirit. Ask the spirits to bless your Medicine Wheel. Then leave the wheel. The ceremony is concluded.

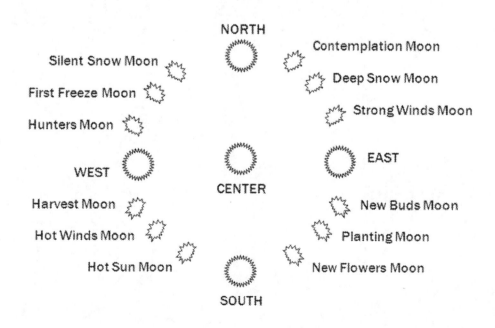

SELECTED REFERENCES

Cornelio, Marie Williams. *Gemstones and Color*. West Hartford, Connecticut: The Triad Publishing Company, 1985.

Doore, Gary. *Shaman's Path, Healing, Personal Growth and Empowerment*. Boston: Shambhala Publications, Inc., 1988.

Grey Wolf. *Earth Signs: How to Connect with the Natural Spirits of the Earth*. New York: Daybreak Books, 1998.

Melody. *Love is in the Earth, a Kaleidoscope of Crystals*. Wheat Ridge, Colorado: Earth-Love Publishing House, 1995.

Prata, Kathleen R. *Symbols, Guiding Lights Along the Journey of Life*. A.R.E. Membership Series. Virginia Beach, Virginia: A.R.E. Press, 1997.

Samuels, Michael M.D. and Mary Rockwood Lane, Ph.D. *The Path of the Feather*. New York: G.P. Putnam's Sons, 2000.

Sun Bear, Wabun Wind, and Crysalis Mulligan. *Dancing with the Wheel: The Medicine Wheel Workbook*. New York: Fireside, 1991.

Sun Bear and Wabun. *The Medicine Wheel, Earth Astrology*. New York: Prentice Hall Press, 1980.

http://www.geocities.com/RainForest/Canopy/1835/wheel.html

http://www.medicinewheel.com

http://www.solar-center.stanford/edu/AO/bighorn.html

http://www.sootribe.org/medicinewheel.html

ABOUT THE AUTHOR

Kathy L. Callahan, Ph.D.

Kathy L. Callahan, Ph.D., was born in Chicago, Illinois. She received a bachelor's degree from the University of Illinois at Chicago Circle, and a Master of Science degree from Purdue University. As a graduate student, she traveled to Tucson, Arizona, where she conducted research on alcoholism treatment modalities for urban Tohono O'Odham (Papago Indians), for which she earned a Ph.D. in 1981, also from Purdue University. She has also lived on the Laguna Pueblo Reservation in New Mexico. She was commissioned as an officer in the U.S. Navy in 1982, and has served as a career Naval officer since that time. She is currently stationed in Washington, D.C.

Kathy has been a student of the Edgar Cayce readings for over 40 years, and strives to actively apply the principles found in the readings in her daily life. She has been a student of *A Course in Miracles* for 20 years and is also a certified Stephen Minister. A very compelling speaker and trainer, Kathy teaches courses and workshops on a variety of subjects including the Universal Laws. She has presented seminars at A.R.E. Headquarters and field conferences, and has appeared on radio and television. The author of several books, she is currently working on a biblical fiction book entitled *Ruth: Sister of the Master*. Kathy currently resides in Burke, Virginia with her family.

Deirdre L. Aragon

Deirdre L. Aragon is a Laguna Pueblo Indian, who spent the early years of her life on the Laguna Pueblo Reservation in New Mexico. Her paternal grandmother and aunt, who were tribal healers, taught Deirdre the wisdom and teachings of her tribe. She was raised in a home where metaphysical principles and holistic healing were accepted and practiced as a way of life. During a near death experience when she was ten years old, Deirdre was given the "mark of the shaman" from the spirit world. Accepting her abilities, Deirdre has designed several healing techniques based on her personal experiences and knowledge gained through various sources.

Deirdre has participated in A.R.E. Search for God Study Groups since she was a child. As a young adult she helped facilitate a group in the Midwest and often held small workshops on the Study Group program and the A.R.E. She was first asked to speak about her near-death experience at an A.R.E New Years Youth Conference in 1995. Although this was an informal meeting it was a memorable experience. Adding to her spiritual growth Deirdre has been a student of the Unity Movement for over 18 years. Deirdre currently resides in Burke, Virginia with her family.

Noble Minds

---

www.noble-minds.com

Noble Minds is dedicated to the promotion of personal spiritual growth and physical wellness in everyday life. We believe that there is one Creative Force but that there are many paths to Truth. We strive to be but one light on that path. We are aware of the challenges of everyday life, and hope to act as a companion to others as we make the spiritual journey together. We offer health services and educational programs as tools to create a positive lifestyle.

The health services offered by Deirdre L. Aragon are based on American Indian healing traditions of the Laguna Pueblo. The educational programs offered by Deirdre and Kathy L. Callahan, Ph.D. are based on the Edgar Cayce readings, Unity principles, world religions and other metaphysical beliefs and practices.

As you review the pages of our website you will have the opportunity to learn more about Noble Minds and our dedication to helping others. We strive to be a companion on the path of enlightenment and we look forward to seeing you on the journey.

Blessings and Joy,
Deirdre & Kathy